ADVANCE PRAISE FOR

# Practicing Futures: A Civic Imagination Action Handbook

"From the global pandemic to climate change, looming crises urge us to pause and take an opportunity to imagine and then create a better world. But how do we take that first step of imagining a world that truly breaks free into a possible future? With advice both practical and inspirational, *Practicing Futures* shows us how."

—Elyse Eidman-Aadahl,
Executive Director of the National Writing Project

"Motivating communities to imagine a just future is a powerful act of building solidarity. And yet, it is hard work to create intentional spaces for collaborative play and visioning, to bring people together to engage in deep listening and ideation on the path to shaping a better world. In *Practicing Futures: A Civic Imagination Action Handbook*, authors Sangita Shresthova and Gabriel Peters-Lazaro beautifully bring to life the hard work involved in inspiring collective civic imagination, taking us along on journeys of dreaming and discovery, letting us in on the 'why' and 'how to' details of fueling social change through the radical process of finding creative communion with our fellow humans."

—Caty Borum Chattoo, Executive Director of the Center
for Media & Social Impact; Author of *Story Movements:
How Documentaries Empower People and Inspire Social Change*,
and Co-author of *A Comedian and an Activist Walk Into a Bar:
The Serious Role of Comedy in Social Justice*

"It is all too rare to find a book this widely researched, richly theorized, and immensely practical for all of us who seek to imagine together what our shared world can be. I can't think of a more timely or crucial contribution to civic life and learning."

—Lissa Soep, Executive Producer of Journalism + Innovation Lab
and Founding Director at YRMedia

# Practicing Futures

new
literacies
q

AND DIGITAL EPISTEMOLOGIES

Colin Lankshear and Michele Knobel
*General Editors*

Vol. 83

The New Literacies and Digital Epistemologies series
is part of the Peter Lang Education list.
Every volume is peer reviewed and meets
the highest quality standards for content and production.

PETER LANG
New York • Bern • Berlin
Brussels • Vienna • Oxford • Warsaw

Gabriel Peters-Lazaro and Sangita Shresthova

# Practicing Futures

# A Civic Imagination Action Handbook

PETER LANG
New York • Bern • Berlin
Brussels • Vienna • Oxford • Warsaw

Library of Congress Cataloging-in-Publication Data

Names: Peters-Lazaro, Gabriel, author. | Shresthova, Sangita, author.
Title: Practicing futures: a civic imagination action handbook /
Gabriel Peters-Lazaro, Sangita Shresthova.
Description: New York: Peter Lang, 2020.
Series: New literacies and digital epistemologies; vol. 83 | ISSN 1523-9543
Includes bibliographical references and index.
Identifiers: LCCN 2020022427 (print) | LCCN 2020022428 (ebook)
ISBN 978-1-4331-6180-3 (hardback) | ISBN 978-1-4331-7270-0 (paperback)
ISBN 978-1-4331-7267-0 (ebook pdf) | ISBN 978-1-4331-7268-7 (epub)
ISBN 978-1-4331-7269-4 (mobi)
Subjects: LCSH: Imagination. | Social change. | Civics.
Classification: LCC BF408 .P399 2020 (print) | LCC BF408 (ebook) |
DDC 303.48/4—dc23
LC record available at https://lccn.loc.gov/2020022427
LC ebook record available at https://lccn.loc.gov/2020022428
DOI 10.3726/b15998


Bibliographic information published by **Die Deutsche Nationalbibliothek**.
**Die Deutsche Nationalbibliothek** lists this publication in the "Deutsche
Nationalbibliografie"; detailed bibliographic data are available
on the Internet at http://dnb.d-nb.de/.

Dedication

For Robyn, who always helps me see the way. - Gabriel Peters-Lazaro

For Marek and Amish, who inspire me to see the world in new ways.
-Sangita Shresthova

# Table of Contents

# Figures

# Foreword: The Work of Imagining Communities

HENRY JENKINS

Today, our popular memories see the 1940s as a golden age for civic engagement in America. The Second World War brought the United States together around a common cause—to overcome fascism, to make the world safe for democracy—and returning home, the "Greatest Generation" sought to build a stronger, more affluent, more forward-thinking country. These were the "good old days" in many of today's narratives of civic decline. But, writing in the post-war period, political scientist George B. Huszar (1945) worried that the nation might soon experience the kind of "disintegration" of democratic culture which enabled the rise of dictators in Europe and Japan. And this was because democracy had become a thing of words rather than actions. Huszar writes in his 1945 book, *Practical Applications of Democracy*, "Democracy is something you do; not something you talk about. It is more than a form of government, or an attitude or opinion. It is participation." (xiii)

Huszar made a core distinction between "talk-democracy" and "do-democracy," arguing that democracy should be embedded into the practices of everyday life. Talk-Democracy, he suggests, is often top-down, as people consent to being governed by people who are all too ready to tell us what to do: "The teacher tells it to the children, the preacher tells it to the congregation, the employer tells it to his employees, and the politician tells it to the voters. We add together all this telling and call it democracy." (12) But, "Do-Democracy" emerges from "creative participation by intelligent human beings in the ongoing process of society." He concluded "The problem of democracy is not merely how to obtain consent, but also, how to create opportunities for participation and a determination to participate." (13) His goal was to create "warm, personal, satisfying human relationships that develop when men join together in groups" that are empowered to take meaningful action on decisions that directly impact their lives (17).

Looking backwards, scholars of civic engagement, such as Robert Putnam (2000), point to the bowling leagues, garden clubs, Parent-Teacher Associations, and other civic organizations as helping to foster a sense of neighborliness and meaningful participation during this post-war era which they argue has been lost in more recent years. Huszar embraces similar groups, particularly those like the PTA which work together to solve shared problems: "The problem-centered-group is democratic in structure; it leads to the preservation of the integrity of the individual, nourishes his productive powers, and encourages participation. This structure is flexible, informal, stimulating and creative, with participant leadership. In contrast, the authoritarian social structure is rigid, formal, regimented, hierarchical, noncreative, and frustrating to the individual, with 'leadership' from the top down." (26) Though largely forgotten today, Huszar's concepts of "talk-democracy" and "do-democracy" have enormous relevance for our own time, where many are similarly worried about the disintegration of core democratic institutions and practices, the breakdown of civic ties within local communities, and a decline in our sense that there is any common ground to be identified amidst the sharp ideological divides between the country's two competing political parties.

To be clear, Huszar's "problem-centered groups" can only move forward with a great deal of talking, exchanging ideas, identifying shared values, swapping stories, forging shared vocabularies, proposing solutions, and debating the merits of different plans. But, he sees such talk as emerging among equals who understand themselves as empowered to participate, who are encouraged to contribute, and who have some expectation that their ideas will be respected by the others in their community. In a community with strong civic engagement, these problem-centered discussions may spill over into their everyday interactions—at the barbers, at the hairdressing salon, at the grocery store, at the bowling alley, in the taxi cab, at the coffee shop and tavern (to cite classic examples of civic spaces). Through such exchanges, we accumulate social capital and learn to respect each other as vital members of a shared community. Contemporary political theorist Peter Dahlgren

(2009) makes a similar point: "The looseness, open-endedness of everyday talk, its creativity, its potential for empathy and affective elements, are indispensable resources and preconditions for the vitality of democratic politics." (90)

His idea that civic dialogues pave the way for democratic politics is only partially true. Core distinctions between civics and politics often get elided. The civic represents the shared beliefs and values, the underlying trust, which makes collective action possible, while the political encapsulates struggles over power within the decision-making process. In a well-functioning civic culture, people may disagree, fight hard for what they believe in, and then accept each other back as neighbors, because there is a core democratic infrastructure which allows us to resolve conflicts and agree to disagree so that we may continue to live side by side within a particular community. Sociologist Nina Eliasoph (1998) describes the ways we increasingly avoid politics as a topic in our everyday conversations with people we care about, fearing that political disagreements have become too divisive and that the heated disagreements may fray social ties in the absence of shared civic commitments. Because we lack such mutual understandings, the community fails to come back together again, wounds do not heal, in the wake of elections and other political events. Rather than developing the basis for shared understandings, we end up locked in a permanent culture war. Here, the political destroys the exchanges which enable the civic to persist and it is in that sense that talk-democracy may ultimately result in a loss of civic agency. Right now, democracy needs our help.

*Practicing Futures: a Civic Imagination Action Handbook* can be understood as a workbook for people who want to help rebuild the civic infrastructure of American democracy, who are interested in how they might *do* democracy at the local level within their own community. It describes ways communities might come together to consider alternatives to current conditions, to imagine what a better future might look like, and to build worlds together that help them to articulate shared values, hopes, and dreams. Through these workshops, we often find the common ground that so often seems missing in more partisan political discussions. We rediscover social bonds, because we are taking a step sideways from the immediate problems and playing with possibilities together. Imagine that.

A tradition of academic writing has spoken about "imagined communities": the term comes from Benedict Anderson (1983) but he captures something which is widely recognized—the ways a group of people too large to know each other directly perceives each other's presence, feels connected with each other, and comes to share a common history, identity, and vision for the future. Anderson's "imagined" is framed in the past tense, as if what links a group of people together to form, in his case, a nation-state is something which happened a long time ago, something we inherit from generations that preceded us. Often, the images we use to depict democracy—the *Spirit of 1776* or Norman Rockwell's *Four Freedoms*, to cite two examples—are images that evoke a sense of tradition, rooting democracy in the past, rather than as a living tradition. Yet, over time, those old symbols of shared identities and experiences wear out, they become stale as we see them used in far too many President's Day themed advertisements—they become "talk-democracy". We stop listening as leaders talk down and talk past us with empty phrases and dead metaphors.

The work of the Civic Imagination Project embraces a different concept—that of the imagining community which is actively generating new cultural symbols to describe our relationship with each other. Imagination is seen not as a product or a possession (not a fixed identity or predetermined set of contents). Rather, we talk about imagining as a process. Imagination is not something we consume or inherit but something we actively produce together, something we do. We can watch imagining happen; we can hear the voices of people engaged in acts of imagining. We are in the room where it happens. Much like Huszar's "problem-oriented groups," these workshops create the preconditions for democratic imagining, we are constructing a space and claiming a time for active, creative, participation. This book describes some of the processes and practices which help free us to imagine together.

For those who have been on the front lines, making change happen on the ground, all of this talk of "imagining" together may seem loosy-goosy and frankly, beside the point. They want us to do, do, do, because the problems are too immediate, the stakes too high, the resources (chief among them time and energy) are too limited. Imagining, we are sometimes told, is a distraction—mere escapism. The civic imagination may seem all talk and no action. Yet, the work of freeing the imagination is transformative, it paves the way for meaningful action, it opens a space where those who have not yet committed to a specific agenda can work through options together, it allows otherwise opposing groups to find a path forward together.

Social Activist Naomi Klein (2017) has written about her own experiences of sitting in a room with people of diverse backgrounds and concerns, groups that are often set apart and pitted against each other as they fight to be heard amongst the many distractions of a media saturated environment: "We had come together to figure out what connects the crises facing us, and to try to chart a holistic vision for the future ... We also had come together out of a belief that overcoming these divisions—finding and strengthening the threads that run through the various issues and movements—is our most pressing task .... Our goal, and it wasn't modest, was to map not just the world we don't want but the one we want instead." (232–233)

We embrace these same goals through our workshops, whatever groups we are working within and across.

Frankly, we have more work to do in terms of creating truly inclusive spaces around these workshops, tending to operate so far in relation with pre-existing communities with shared histories and beliefs, rather than seeking to bridge differences in the radical and transformative way Klein describes. As a research team, we are actively seeking out and talking with diverse groups but we have not yet brought truly diverse people into the room at the same time. But, then, that is the struggle of the current decade—to overcome histories of discrimination and exclusion, to learn to listen to a broader range of voices, to bring more diverse perspectives to the table. Huszar's "problem-centered-groups" and Putnam's bowling leagues were never as inclusive as our nostalgic celebration of the past might lead us to imagine, and we need to figure out ways to define communities other than through acts of exclusion. We are not going to get past such problems if we cannot learn to talk across our differences. Such exchanges will push us beyond empty talk about "civility" or "political correctness," because they will proceed on the basis of shared understandings and trust. Sometimes, these conversations will be difficult, they require those who have felt left out to call out that history and question its logic, and some people—perhaps many—will get upset in the process. But we can only proceed when we start with a commitment to work through this together, to stick it out through the discomfort in hopes of getting to the other side. And even when these discussions are not as inclusive as we might hope, they do important work in our efforts to build a more just society. As Dahlgren (2009) discusses in relation to the notion of counter-publics, "To work out counterprojects ... often requires some kind of temporary public withdrawal, an internal working through among like-minded citizens .... Attaining new values, defining new needs, and developing new social visions is difficult to attain via consensus-oriented conversation, with universalists assumptions." (90) So, there are times when a smaller, more homogeneous group needs to take stock of where it stands and what it will stand for, just as there are also times when the boundaries of the community need to broaden to incorporate a larger, more diverse mix of participants.

Sangita Shresthova and Gabriel Peters-Lazaro are the authors and architects of the approach described in this book, an approach which has emerged from our research together but which they have taken into the field and refined in partnership with a broad array of stakeholders. Over the past few years, as the principal investigator for the Civic Imagination Project, I have had a chance to observe these techniques in practice, as our research team has tested this approach in communities across America and around the world. We have conducted these workshops with participants ranging in age from middle schoolers to senior citizens, in labor halls and mosques, with policy makers and journalists, students and congregants, all of whom have things they wanted to share with us and especially with each other. I have seen what happens when you bring a group of people together in a room to share stories of memorable objects, to build a world, to create narratives that anticipate touch points in the process of social change, to remix favorite stories, or to reimagine their identities, their communities, and their surrounding environment. I have seen these playful tasks sparking social integration, breaking down suspicions, strengthening social bonds, and sparking fellowship and laughter. Agenda setting and mobilization planning can follow, building on the spirit of good will and trust these workshops generate.

Imagining together can yield unexpected insights as we discover common ground that we might previously never have anticipated. I was surprised when a room full of Arab educators and journalists announced their desire for a world where no one—not the government or their neighbors—polices their religious beliefs and practices. I have struggled to understand how a group of former coal miners and tobacco farmers from Kentucky might simultaneously embrace the need for single payer health care and still vote for leaders dead set against such policies in part because they did not trust any of the social institutions powerful enough to deliver the kind of medical insurance they desired. I have been touched when my graduate students reported back on a session with low income middle school kids from Los Angeles whose vision of the future included many things taken for granted today by more affluent people living in their city or that a child begged for a world where there were no "bad drugs." I have listened to faculty and students of a Swedish university describe their desire for a better health care system having already achieved universal access but not necessarily the quality of communication between doctors and patients that maintained human dignity. And perhaps most profoundly, I have seen how the acts of imagining frees so many to think beyond current impasses. Through this process, some of the common tropes of fantasy or science fiction take on new meaning: magic often becomes a metaphor for power, the teleportation system in *Star Trek* helps Americans think about their carbon footprint, Europeans imagine more efficient means of moving across their Union, and Arabs express their fears of the risks refugees face in traveling to other parts of the world. A world which possesses tele-transportation is also a world without border police or fixed boundaries: a world where anyone can beam anywhere at any time without having to show their papers. Sometimes the fantastic allows us to speak about realities too painful to confront otherwise or to imagine possibilities too wonderful to imagine possible.

Every one of these workshops allow us to take soundings of the civic imaginations of particular communities, often finding unexpected common ground both within and between diverse groups of participants. And, these workshops allow communities to come together around common causes, sometimes serving as a springboard for taking action to address long ignored problems and conflicts. Sangita Shresthova and Gabriel Peters-Lazaro share stories of such encounters across this book, so that you, too, can hear the voices, listen to the stories, of people who came together to "imagine better," as J.K. Rowling put it memorably in her 2008 Harvard Graduation Speech. And you can put these ideas into action yourself within your own communities, as you learn how to do democracy, much as community builders did in the immediate post-war era.

So, you think democracy is in crisis. What are we going to do about it? We can only imagine.

# Bibliography

Anderson, Benedict. 1983. *Imagined Communities.* New York: Verso.

Dahlgren, Peter. 2009. *Media and Political Engagement: Citizens, Communication, and Democracy.* Cambridge, UK: Cambridge University Press.

Eliasoph, Nina. 1998. *Avoiding Politics: How Americans Produce Apathy in Everyday Life.* Cambridge, UK: Cambridge University Press.

Huszar, George B. 1945. *Practical Applications of Democracy.* New York: Harper & Brothers.

Klein, Naomi. 2017. *No Is Not Enough: Resisting Trump's Politics and Winning the World We Need.* Chicago: Haymarket Books.

Putnam, Robert. 2000. *Bowling Alone: The Collapse and Revival of American Community.* New York: Simon and Schuster.

Williams, Raymond. 2001. "Culture Is Ordinary." In *The Raymond Williams Reader*, ed. John Higgins, 10–24. London: Blackwell.

# OVERVIEW

This section provides a thematic and conceptual overview of the civic imagination as a framework based on its six key functions, which map a rough pathway from personal to collective empowerment. Each function of the civic imagination reflects our belief that the fictive and the utopian imagination can open up new possibilities for consideration that would not otherwise arise. Our concept of the civic imagination grew from the research and writing of *By Any Media Necessary: the New Youth Activism* (2016) and *Popular Culture and the Civic Imagination: Case Studies of Creative Social Change* (2020). The concept matured and took on a greater sense of focus and urgency when our research group began working to translate the findings of that project into creative participatory interventions.

Having seen the power of creating and harnessing shared story worlds and fantastical narratives as tools of civic engagement in case studies of the Harry Potter Alliance, the DREAMers movement and elsewhere, there was a strong desire to create pedagogic resources that would help other communities harness and adapt such creative practices to their own needs and logics. Our approach to the civic imagination is guided by five conceptual themes that inform both our theoretical and practical work. Civics, imagination, worldbuilding, commitment to participation, and working through "any media" are crucial to the experiences and tools shared in this *Handbook*.

# CHAPTER ONE

# About Practicing Futures

## Introduction

"This is a story about the Vietnam War and Peter Rabbit." So began a story told by a third grader named Sarah.[1] Sarah, an Asian American girl in Los Angeles, had composed the story with a group of her peers as part of a workshop with the Penny Harvest Leadership Academy at the University of Southern California in October of 2018. In their story Peter Rabbit—a well-known character of children's fiction created by Beatrix Potter and featured in a recent animated film adaptation—travels back in time from the present day to find himself in Vietnam in the 1960s. Due to unforeseen circumstances, Peter gets trapped in Northern Vietnam and ends up in jail. He is desolate and filled with despair. Eventually, he is released and permitted to leave. Full of anticipation, he boards a plane that takes him to Los Angeles, where he settles down and begins a happier life. As she finished telling this story, Sarah exhaled with relief and her group mates smiled in encouragement, clearly content with how she had conveyed their work.

Over 60 elementary aged children from nearby schools, including Sarah, participated in our civic imagination workshops as part of Penny Harvest that day. The workshops invited the children to surface and document stories that they felt were

---

1. Names of all participants have been changed to protect their identities.

inspiring. They then worked in small groups to identify characters, themes and plot twists from each of their stories that they could then incorporate into a whole new narrative. This process of collaborative remix was a fun way for students to work creatively together, focusing on story elements that they enjoyed and values that they shared. Sarah's group's story of Peter Rabbit in Vietnam was just one of the many imaginative narratives created that day. Their particular contribution came about from a combination of two of the group members having shared family stories of migration. They then combined those family stories with the story and character of Peter Rabbit, which had been inspirational to a third member of the group because of the rabbit's resilience and ingenuity. Every story produced that day was as original and surprising in its own way as the Peter Rabbit remix. The children drew on stories from diverse perspectives and sources including fiction, popular culture and personal experience in ways that provided a powerful commentary on their concerns and aspirations, about their real lived experiences and their imagined possibilities. The act of sharing stories that mattered to each of them as individuals, and then creating something completely new from that material, provided a framework in which powerful community building and civic agency was given the chance to emerge in accordance with the practice of civic imagination that forms the backbone of this book.

## What Is the Civic Imagination?

For us, the stories that the children created during the Penny Harvest workshop were an exercise of the civic imagination. We define civic imagination as a practice of envisioning social change that supports a movement towards a better world. Civic imagination supports the creation and strengthening of imagined/imagining communities, one's own civic agency, respect and understanding for the perspectives of others, and opportunities for freedom and equality that have not yet been experienced. Our research discovered a range of ways that groups are addressing the need to foster the civic imagination by linking story-making and media-making to their political efforts. One of the most striking practices noted across our case studies included groups tapping the imaginative worlds of popular culture as means of translating and expressing real world social concerns. *Popular Culture and the Civic Imagination: Case Studies of Creative Social Change* (2020, NYU Press), co-edited with Henry Jenkins, shared 30 case studies from authors around the world detailing such practices; from activists remixing images of Smokey Bear to protest the Trump administration to accounts of activist theater in India, to an academic study on the politics around Star Wars fandom. These cases showcase powerful examples of the civic imagination at work in the world. But another important branch of our work has always been about understanding just what civic imagination can DO and how any of us can practice civic imagination for ourselves. And that is exactly what this book project is all about.

Based on our engagement with real world examples, we developed a framework based on six key functions of the civic imagination, providing us with a rough pathway from personal to collective empowerment. Specifically, the civic imagination can help us:

1. **Imagine Ourselves as Civic Agents.** *Connect the imagination to personal and social identities as people think about their own capacities for social action.*
2. **Imagine A Better World.** *Recognize the value of utopian and dystopian narratives for helping people to think about what they are fighting for as well as what they are fighting against.*
3. **Imagine Our Social Connections with a Larger Community.** *See the imagination as central to the formation of collective identities, imagined/imagining communities, and shared histories.*
4. **Bring an Imaginative Dimension to Our Real World Spaces and Places.** *Encourage an interplay between cultural geography, urban space, and the civic imagination.*
5. **Forge Solidarity with Others with Experiences Different from Our Own.** *Identify imagination as crucial to networked connections made by disparate groups during struggles over political change and social justice.*
6. **Imagine the Process of Change.** *Understand that civic action tactics and strategies emerge from activists' ability to imagine a process transformation.*

Each function of the civic imagination reflects our belief that the fictive and the utopian imagination can open up new possibilities for consideration that would not arise if we remain mired in what Stephen Duncombe (2012) describes as "the tyranny of the possible"—the idea that an overemphasis on day-to-day pragmatism can stifle our ability to imagine alternatives and take action towards realizing them. When combined, the functions of the civic imagination allow us to activate the imagination as a crucial step that helps us mobilize, organize and act. As a participant in one of our sessions noted when interviewed, civic imagination can be seen as an approach that invites "an unlimited possibility for improvement—the fact, this idea, that society and culture are within certain existing status quos. But the 'civic imagination' invites us to think beyond those status quos".

## What's in the Handbook?

*Practicing Futures: A Civic Imagination Action Handbook* presents new imaginative tools created for community building, civic engagement, and action planning.

These tools break free of assumptions and definitions that might otherwise trap us in repetitive, rather than productive, cycles of disagreement, inability to compromise and alienation, preventing action and collective aspiration. In other words, this handbook is a practical guide to the civic imagination that supports the development of civically meaningful story worlds and campaigns that can have real world impact. Our workshops are suggestions for those interested in surfacing the civic imagination in community settings.

Although our work arises from an academic context and is engaged with the evolving literature around youth, civics, political engagement and popular culture, this text is not meant to be theoretical in that same vein. Along with Henry Jenkins, we detail the theoretical underpinnings of our work in the introduction to the aforementioned *Popular Culture and the Civic Imagination* (2020). Interested readers should consult that volume and the included recommended reading list at the end of this handbook. The overwhelming focus of this book is to share our practical guide and support the civic imagination in community-based and institutional contexts.

This book was written with a broad range of readers interested in working with the imagination in civic contexts in mind. This includes the educator, the social change advocate, the creative, and the social entrepreneur. Educators who want to expand their approach to civic and other social studies and humanities subjects will be able to pick up our book and directly apply it to their teaching. Our approach is also relevant to people interested in supporting social change among communities. This handbook is really a manual that can be used to jump start the ideation processes for civic action. Our approach might also be useful to creatives who are looking to break out of prescriptive linear narratives and who seek to experiment with story delivery through multiple media platforms. Finally, social entrepreneurs, who seek to connect their branding to socially conscious worldviews, could apply our civic imagination approaches to their strategic thinking.

So, what can you expect from the rest of this handbook? Section Two— 'Practice Chronicles' shares how our approach to civic imagination evolved through formative community engagements and creative collaborations. Each chronicle tells the story of developing and running a workshop within the context of a specific community. These included artists, activists and students collaborating around contemporary issues facing Pakistan, educators and academics convening for conferences, young Latinx students participating in activist training programs, faith-based communities in Arkansas, and more. In each case, it took an active practice of building trust to create an environment in which people could open up and practice imagination together. We share the key insights gained as well as the challenges faced with the hope that what we learned will help anyone engaging civic imagination in practice. This section also shares some more of the surprising, delightful, and inspiring stories that came out of these collaborations, adding to the sum total of civic imagination connected through a vibrant global network that is growing every day.

Section Three—'The Practice Guidebook,' offers workshops to enact a civic imagination practice that is adaptable to a variety of communities, situations and goals. Practices in this section are crafted around the six functions of the civic imagination and range from personal reflections on memory, identity and stories that have been personally inspiring, to large scale community interventions focused on envisioning the world of the future. In all cases, the goal is to surface core values in creative ways that can strengthen individual aspirational visions to facilitate community and coalition building, innovative problem solving and capacity for change.

The real world is full of challenges and the sheer weight of problems facing us can stifle the genius of our human creativity at exactly the time when we desperately need radical and innovative solutions. Utopias and dystopias have long been used to pose questions, provoke discussions, and inspire next steps, and are helpful because they break contemporary frames and encourage long view perspectives.

This book taps into examples and models from our community facing work that supported the creation of shared storyworlds through media-centric approaches deployed in service of civic and political action. It also provides a step-by-step guide to our method with the objective of making it accessible to all interested practitioners.

The remainder of this introduction provides additional context and background situating this work within a long term collaborative framework.

## About Us

We are educators, media practitioners and researchers who engage with connections between culture and politics through scholarly inquiry and community practice. Gabriel is a faculty member of the University of Southern California's School of Cinematic Arts where his approaches to scholarship and creative work are defined by a productive marriage of critical theory and emergent media practices. Sangita is a Research Director for the Civic Paths Group as USC's Annenberg School of Communication and Journalism and has a history that includes dancing professionally and creating media. Along with Henry Jenkins, who authored the foreword to this book, we created and lead the Civic Imagination Project, which maps the civic imagination through research, case studies, workshops and brainstorming sessions with people from diverse grassroots communities.

The Civic Imagination Project resides within the Civic Paths Group at the University of Southern California, which Henry Jenkins and Sangita founded in 2009. Each week in Civic Paths, students, researchers and practitioners meet to discuss contemporary scholarship, work together on conceptual and intervention projects, and provide feedback on one another's projects. On the one hand, the Civic Paths Group has engaged in conceptual work. We have authored publications, hosted numerous talks and conferences, seeded multiple dissertation projects, and otherwise fostered cutting edge discussions about contemporary culture and politics. On the other hand, Civic Paths has also carried out a range of interventions, running workshops and brainstorming sessions with activists, educators, journalists, and policymakers that deploy techniques of world building, storytelling and remix to help them move beyond impasses in the current thinking. These activities have benefited from the long term support of the John D. and Catherine T. MacArthur Foundation. The work has involved collaborations with a range of other organizations, including the Salzburg Academy for Media and Global Change, the National Writing Project, the National Association for Media Literacy Educators, Facing History and Ourselves, CDF Freedom Schools, the Good Shepherd Lutheran Church, the Muslim Public Affairs Council, Project Zero, Penny Harvest Leadership Academy, and the Connected Learning Network. Other partners include those we have brought into our expanded network as speakers and advisors at our public-facing events.

At its core, Civic Paths brings together researchers and practitioners interested in the intersection between cultural studies and political change through the lens of participatory culture, which we, like Henry Jenkins, define as "a diverse set of shared activities and social engagements, ranging from fan fiction writing and crafting to gaming, through which people collectively carve out a space for expression and learning." In his earlier work, Jenkins (2016) described participatory culture practices as those that have "relatively low" barriers to expression and engagement, "strong social support for creating and sharing," a shared sense that all contributions matter, and informal opportunities for mentorship and training for interested participants. In Civic Paths, we often speak of culture and civics as connecting through a range of practices that we associate with participatory cultures.

Our current work on the civic imagination is an outgrowth of our multi-year involvement with the MacArthur Youth and Participatory Politics Network, which defined participatory politics as "interactive, peer-based acts through which individuals and groups seek to exert both voice and influence on issues of public concern" (Cohen and Kahne 2012, 3). Participatory politics also connects cultural networks, skills and practices to engagement in civic and political spaces. Our team's contribution to the work of the YPP Network, summarized in the 2016 book, *By Any Media Necessary: The New Youth Activism*, focused on the following five 'exemplar' case studies of innovative networks and organizations that recruit, train, and mobilize young activists: Invisible Children (the organization behind the infamous Kony2012 video), the Harry Potter Alliance (a nonprofit that translates Harry Potter stories into real world civic action), the DREAMer movement (made up of youth mobilized around immigration reform), Students for Liberty (a college organization that supports college-aged libertarians), and a range of projects supporting the American Muslim community.

The research presented in *By Any Media Necessary* highlighted the multiple—and at times fraught—trajectories, as young people harness expressive practices (voice) to affect social change (influence). On one hand, young activists had to overcome enormous difficulties in gaining access to the means of cultural production and circulation. Since then we have seen some of them succeed in making their collective voice heard through their innovative use of social media. On the other hand, we also saw youth get frustrated after they attempted to use available tools and failed to have their voice heard. Our research detailed how some groups have access to the skills, knowledge, resources, and social connections that enable them to exert their voice. Others—especially those economically deprived, socially marginalized, historically disempowered—do not. Technological advances have lowered the barriers to producing and circulating media, but they have not yet confronted the systemic and structural obstacles that block certain voices from being heard and listened to and that may continue to elevate the voices that have historically been the loudest.

Despite their many differences, the communities included in our case study research were effective in harnessing inspiring stories to build and support communities that could then be mobilized to take action. As we explored the narratives that resonated and how they operated within these participatory communities, we noted that that they provided a sense of future, a forward momentum, that also recognized the value of the past. These narratives sustained and supported groups, many of which relied on networked organizational structures and social media to mobilize and sustain their civic imagination.

## Key Concepts

Our approach is guided by five conceptual themes that inform both our theoretical and practical work. Civics, imagination, worldbuilding, commitment to participation, and working through "any media" are crucial to the workshops shared in this handbook.

## Civics

In the foreword to this book, Henry Jenkins provides an extended exploration and definition of civics as it relates to our work. To reiterate here, civic engagement is the process by which communities establish a shared set of values that in turn support the functions and structures of democracy. Democracy requires participation to function. It requires that the members of a community feel that their views and voices count and that they are investing in a system that values them. When there are diverse structures and activities creating opportunities for civic engagement, politics can play a productive and valuable role in public life. Politics is an adjunct to civics, a milieu in which negotiations and struggles over power take place. When civic foundations are threatened or weak, politics becomes a battle of alienation. Right now we see such utter divisiveness in the political process at all scales from local to global that there is a real lack of shared vision and values. Yet when people do find ways to come together and listen to each other they learn that the things that unite and connect them are stronger and more various than those that divide. This is what we have found in our workshops all over the country and around the world. What's lacking is opportunity and language.

In so many cases, the language of shared values is already co-opted and infused with political rhetoric. Civic imagination gives us a way to explore new visions that align with our ideals and ways of expressing them through the practices of imagination and the language of speculative fiction.

## Imagination to Imagining

We believe the imagination should (indeed needs to) be a key dimension of our civic lives. We also recognize that the socio-economic and other challenges faced by many communities are also real and require real mobilization and action. In fact, we saw ample evidence of the important role that the act of imagining played in supporting such civic action through our earlier work on civic engagement (through the MAPP Project) . The civic imagination also helped build a sense of community and through this sustained engagement. The Harry Potter Alliance (HPA), a group founded by Harry Potter fans who wanted to translate the love of Harry Potter to real world action, is the quintessential example of imaginative civic action.

Over the course of our research, the HPA harnessed the imagination towards real world action again and again as they extended narrative tropes from the Harry Potter content world to the real world. In one particularly visible campaign, the enslavement of the house-elves in the books became a rallying cry for the fans as they launched the "Not in Harry's Name" campaign to pressure Warner Brothers to only use Fair Trade products in the chocolates they marketed alongside the Harry Potter movie releases.

As we delved further into literature that surrounds the imagination as a human facility, we noted that its importance has been amply noted by creative and critical thinkers. We have been particularly drawn to the work of philosopher, educator and social change advocate Maxine Greene, who stresses that the imagination is BOTH an individual AND collective practice, which provides us with the "felt possibility of looking beyond the boundary where the backyard ends or the road narrows, diminishing out of sight" (Greene 1995, 26). In her articulation of the imagination, Greene draws on the work of John Dewey, Emily Dickinson and Mary Warnock among others to piece together an argument for the imagination as a "gateway" (Dewey 1934, pg. 272 in Greene 20) that helps us bridge between the past and future to expand our notion of the what is possible, beyond what may seem reasonable. Greene also draws on Mary Warnock to extend imagination outwards, beyond the personal to share and connect creatively with others. Connecting this notion of the imagination to Paulo Freire's observation that "Hopelessness is a form of silence, of denying the world and fleeing from it", the imagination becomes an integral element of hope and an important, in fact necessary, dimension of civic action (Freire 80 in Greene 24).

Our workshops invite participants to engage in the process of imagining and through this create a temporary space akin to the potentially transformative "green world" described by Shakespearean scholars (Frye 1957; Forker 1985). In the green world, characters temporarily exit the constraints and rigid boundaries of everyday life to renew themselves and their relationships. They do this by literally and metaphorically transporting themselves to another place (in this case nature). They then return refreshed, sometimes even transformed, able to tackle the challenges they must face.

Though clearly different in many ways, our civic imagination workshops aim to create a temporary space similar to the "green world" in so far as they invite participants to gather and collectively take a break from their everyday lives to remember what is important, share with each other, and imagine aspirational future worlds. Our hope, confirmed by our experiences running workshops for the past five years, is that participants are able to return to their daily lives with renewed vigor and shared commitment. For us, imagining is an action. It is not escapism.

## Worldbuilding

A central aspect of our methodology is that of worldbuilding, which, as Laura Cechanowicz, Brian Cantrell, and Alex McDowell (2016, 29) summarize is an approach that supports a "myriad of stories by multiple storytellers across disparate platforms—including those platforms that may not yet be named." Instead of following traditional storytelling models centered around a single author producing individual creative works, the worldbuilding process focuses on harnessing the creative energies of invested groups to conjure shared visions of complete worlds and then empower them to find and share stories within those worlds. Those stories might then take multiple forms—novels, comics, games, Virtual Reality, audio dramas, etc.—but will all draw on the common lore engendered by the creative community. This reorganization of the creative process opens up opportunities for innovative partnerships amongst groups that might not traditionally work together. Be they social justice activists and creative professionals or community organizers and elementary school students, a civic imagination practice informed by worldbuilding methodologies provides a nimble and exciting framework for collaboration.

We use participatory worldbuilding to engage communities in a process that invites them to think about what alternative worlds might look like, reading them in relation to our own, and deploying them as a means of expressing and debating visions for what alternatives might be to current conditions. This frees participants from the challenges on the imagination which are posed by a relentless focus on existing constraints which limit the possibilities for change, resulting in activists self-censoring themselves, rather than brainstorming the full range of possible directions they could go. Some political veterans in our partner organizations have been initially skeptical of what they saw as the 'escapist' dimensions of our approach, but they have often rethought this opposition when they saw how this approach re-energized participants.

## Participation and Process

Our workshops aim to create supportive environments in which participants nurture their own and their collective imaginative voices through participation. Through shared narrative construction participants gain a sense of the powerful potential that storytelling holds for real world change. As facilitators we offer creative constraints and an overall sense of progression and workflow, so that at each stage of learning, participants are able to engage fully in the imaginative work at hand. This work includes free-wheeling brainstorms about the contours and qualities of shared imaginary worlds and work in smaller groups. The focus is on the process rather than the product. We give hints, suggestions and time limits for each creative stage, but maintain an open sensibility as to what the deliverable is, so long as it serves the story.

If, in the course of a workshop, we arrive at the point that a group's story will be translated into media (having evolved from a spoken and then performed idea), we spend only a little time going over the 'basics'—here's the on button, here's the lens, keep your subject in the frame, get the mic as close as you can, make sure you get all the parts of the story that you need, and then go for it. Each group then finds their own way to make their movie. Some participants enter into these activities having already had some experiences with video making, but many come without. Everyone has been comfortable with the tools and excited to engage in the practices. Participants discover for themselves, from necessity and logic, how to shoot coverage of a scene, run it in a wide shot then go in for close ups and reverses. It is a powerful moment when you figure out for yourself how continuity editing works and the veil of movie magic lifts. It is more powerful, in our experience, than trying to explain all of these things before hand, in the abstract, as though they are hard and fast rules that will make or break a project. When participants struggle, we give support and guidance, but try to let them figure things out for themselves as much as possible.

In this way, the practices of media production are a more direct extension of the creative impetus from which they grow. The resulting media products then serve as a basis for reflection, discussion and further creative and collective growth. Participants see and share their successes and mistakes, fueling a cycle of creative iteration and refinement as we maintain a facilitator role that values participation and minimal intervention.

## By Any Media

Our approach is rooted in a praxis of creative expression and cultural remixing. Drawing on our earlier work, we also stress that media production can happen through "any media necessary". Our approach is rooted in the notion of the "participation gap"—defined as "the unequal access to the opportunities, experiences, skills, and knowledge that will prepare youth for the world of tomorrow" (Jenkins 2006, 3–4)—and our work with communities that struggle to achieve social change despite such inequalities. While skill mastery matters when it comes to media production, the ability to tap the imagination, express ideas, and connect to others is a crucial first step to producing media that is meaningful and resonant. Specific skill development can then respond to needs identified during the creative process. We encourage young people to be aware of the expressive possibilities available to them and use them to achieve their goals. To summarize, access to media technologies and skill development matter; so do expressive freedom and young people's sense of agency when it comes to creating and sharing media.

Combining these concepts, our approach to 'practicing' the civic imagination centers on the creation of new tools for community building, civic engagement and action planning through a harnessing of shared values and tapping the boundless potential of human imagination to break free of assumptions and definitions that might otherwise trap us in repetitive cycles of disagreement and alienation, preventing progress and collective aspiration. Our materials draw on our ongoing engagement with the civic imagination in practice and build on our sustained conversations with activists, educators, journalists and policymakers that deploy techniques of worldbuilding, storytelling and remix to help them move beyond impasses in the current thinking.

## Our Journey

> "The thing that I really love about the design of this is that you're considering life on earth and then you're engaging people through imagination and creativity about future problems but also future solutions. And that requires listening and building consensus and then making something together …. It exercises all the tools you need to really ever do anything in this life."
>
> Visual artist reflecting on her workshop participation in 2017

A visual artist and community organizer shared this understanding of the civic imagination in the aftermath of the Imagine 2040 event we organized in Los Angeles on April 20, 2017, which brought together a diverse group, made up of artists, academics, creative workers, designers, and activists to collectively reflect on our approach to the civic imagination. Though it was one of many civic imagination focused workshops we have run over the past few years, Imagine 2040 marked an important moment for our work. It was the first time we shared our approach and questions with such a diverse and knowledgeable group. It was also a crucial moment where we took stock of what we had learned already, what we had accomplished. It was also the moment when we committed to developing a set of accessible tools that anyone could use to support the civic imagination in their communities.

Drawing on real world examples and workshops we had piloted with affiliated communities, the Imagine 2040 event allowed us to share our conviction that imagining needs to be an important, perhaps crucial, dimension of our civic lives. As we watched participants' future visions emerge and listened to their feedback on the opportunities and challenges that our approach presented, we were overwhelmed with a sense that our work on the civic imagination matters, and matters a lot at this particular moment when divisiveness and contention dominate our political discourse even as the wide consensus is that the stakes are high. Populations displaced by war and environmental disaster; apocalyptic fears linked to the COVID-19 pandemic, deep divides within national electorates; a growing sense of urgency for new kinds of civic engagement and political empowerment to take on these challenges, set a course for the future, and create opportunities for new languages and visions of politics.

We are particularly inspired by the work of Czech dissident playwright and former president, Václav Havel who made a powerful case for hope during the height of the Cold War when he wrote:

> Hope, in this deep and powerful sense, is not the same as joy that things are going well, or willingness to invest in enterprises that are obviously headed for early success, but rather an ability to work for something because it is good, not just because it stands a chance to succeed. The more unpromising the situation in which we demonstrate hope, the deeper that hope is. Hope is not the same thing as optimism. It is not the conviction that something will turn out well, but the certainty that something makes sense, regardless of how it turns out." (Havel, *Disturbing the Peace*)

Building on this work, nurturing hope and the imagination is not a luxury, it is a necessity that goes to the very core of what makes us human.

As detailed in the Chronicle section of this book, we ran our first civic imagination workshops in 2013 when we worked with the Islamic Center of Southern California and the Children's Defense Fund Freedom Schools. Though they shared many similarities—they both worked with young in the LA area and endeavored to support their civic identities—the two programs were also quite different.

The youth affiliated with the Islamic Center were all, in one way or another, working to reconcile their politicized American and Muslim identities in a post 9/11 United States. We planned a week-long summer workshop with approximately 30 youth attendees ranging from elementary to high school-aged. From our group's previous research, we knew that in a post 9/11 world this community was forced to grapple with political identity and entanglement merely by virtue of being Muslim in the U.S. We knew that we wanted to run a very creative workshop that would include creating the outlines of a shared fantastical future world, developing narratives that took place in that world, and then guiding the students through the creation of short video vignettes that told their stories. But, we assumed that we would need to frame and orient this work within the political realities and concerns of the community. We felt that we would need to address and center those issues from the beginning, almost as if to justify the subsequent creative activities we had planned.

On the first day of the program we were surprised when our initial future world brainstorm with the youth conspicuously didn't surface any mention of their American Muslim identities. Instead, we were soon surrounded by elements of fantastically playful worlds where flying carpets filled the sky and cows could really jump over the moon. As we reflected on that first day, the group youth coordinator made an important observation about the burden of the overly politicized American Muslim identity that these young people lived every day. She noted that what they really needed was a space and opportunity to let their creativity soar unfettered; they needed time in which imagination comes first. We took this advice to heart and leapt into a week of wild creativity, worldbuilding, storytelling and media making. The experience is detailed in the first entry of our "Chronicles" section. The fictional work of the American Muslim youth participants provided a vehicle for tough conversations with just enough distance from the real world to open up new avenues for understanding. We could never have engineered this exchange directly. The experience was revelatory and set an important foundation for the work moving forward. To start with the imagination, to let fantasy run wild and trust that the values and concerns of the real world will always work their way back in. But by arriving at them through imagination, we might see them anew and perhaps chip away at their power to shape the contours of our thinking.

Later that same summer, our second workshop session with the CDF Freedom School—a social justice focused program serving youth from under-resourced communities—presented us a connected but very distinct context. The high school youth in the program shared a strong commitment to activism, particularly around issues related to immigration reform. For them our workshop offered an invitation to introduce imagination and a moment of collective playfulness into the ways in which they approached the real world challenges they sought to address. Details of this experience can be found in the second entry of the "Chronicles" section.

Bringing our workshop to these two groups so early on in our work on the civic imagination crucially informed our approach. We had to work with the communities to connect our workshop method to the participants' contexts and realities. This was not going to be a one size fits all approach. At the same time, planning the sessions with leaders from both the programs at the table convinced us that our approach to the civic imagination had something meaningful to contribute. This customizable and community-based approach became foundational to our commitment to designing and running workshops.

Throughout the project, we made it a priority to run workshops with as many groups as possible and learned something new about our approach every time. People concerned about the future of work in Bowling Green, Kentucky taught us that we need to respect and honor the past even as we encourage people to imagine the future. In Fayetteville, Arkansas, a Lutheran congregation to considered how faith and organized religion could support a future world where diversity and humanity prevail. Young people affiliated with Youth Radio (now YR Media) in Oakland, California drew our attention to the limitations that the imperatives associated with issue-based activism can place on the imagination. The Arab educators we met in Beirut, Lebanon embraced the theatrical elements of our workshop with enthusiasm that we rarely encountered in other regions. Undergraduate students at the Salzburg Academy for Media and Global Change were drawn to both utopian and dystopian popular culture narratives as they created their shared future worlds.

Combined, the more than 30 workshops we facilitated and the many others we supported developed and tested dynamic set of tools for creative workshops that activate civic imagination. These tools are adaptable to a variety of local contexts and logics and can serve multiple purposes from community and network building to idea generation and media campaign design. In all cases, the founding principle is to address any community's need to see challenges in new ways, ignite creativity, form deep personal engagements with the work, and harness the expansive capacity for imagination within all of us.

Growing out of these experiences with communities in the United States and internationally, civic imagination workshops present specific guidelines that are responsive to local realities.

## Tips

Over the years, we adopted practice conventions that apply to all our workshops. These conventions are essentially process tips that help us get to know a community and encourage a sharing of ideologies, assumptions, opportunities and barriers related to individual and collective civic identities. Building on these exchanges, the workshops invite participants to think beyond these current realities by activating their collective imaginations. As a filmmaker and professor noted during our Imagine 2040 event, "one of the more powerful things of the civic imagination is that it invites us to reconstruct our political structures and our power systems".

We share these conventions here as tips for facilitators who can consider them alongside the local knowledge they have of their participants' communities. The tips are more conceptual and general in nature. Specific tactical tips pertaining to workshop flow are provided in the facilitator guidelines section of this Handbook.

**It really is about the journey.** All our workshops stress the importance of process. We see bringing people together to surface, share and activate the imagination as a crucial dimension of civic lives. While some of our workshops do include suggestions on ways that people may be able to move the narratives and ideas generated through the workshops forward after the activity ends, we also recognize that experiencing the workshop is essential to the civic imagination journey as we see it.

**Be sure to listen. Really Listen.** We enter every workshop setting with our eyes and ears wide open. As soon as we enter a space, we notice how it is set up, where participants have seated themselves. We observe how they are relating to each other. Do they seem to know each other well? Do we note body language that communicates hesitation or concern? We make it a point to approach at least some of the participants before the workshop starts to introduce ourselves briefly and to get an initial sense of the participants' background and motivations. As we go through the ice-breaker, we also focus on what the participants are saying and how they are saying it. We notice how other participants respond.

**Commit to diversity and include a broad range of issues.** We have found that encouraging diverse perspectives to surface is incredibly enriching for the participants. With that in mind, we often go out of our way to extend friendly invitations to participants that initially seem more reserved. Though we generally rely on our workshop participants to generate the content that drives the workshop, we do make selective suggestions if we feel the conversation is becoming too polarized, focused or one sided early into the workshop.

**Allow civics and politics to surface in unexpected ways.** Our workshops bring the imagination to participants' civic lives and communities. In that spirit, we intentionally do not enter through politics. Rather, we enter through an exploration of stories and narratives that the participants find meaningful and inspiring. We believe these stories provide a starting place that invites us to see the human (rather than politically tinted) versions of ourselves, which can then help us see our civic and political lives in new ways, outside of the divisions that define our current formal political debates.

**Make participation less daunting.** Finding and telling compelling stories that convince people to take action can be elusive. Producing a polished media product can be intimidating. Getting stories to spread is challenging. Valuing all levels of participation and allowing people to value their imagination is crucial. Though they vary in their specifics, we structure each of our workshops to help participants feel that they can participate and take action around issues that they care about. Civic engagement is a process and people can participate in ways that make sense to them. In that context, reflecting on the process is just as, if not more important than, achieving the goals young people set for themselves.

**Note popular culture.** In our experience, popular culture informs our imaginations in many ways. For some participants, narratives rooted in popular culture provide sources of inspiration. For other participants, they are sources of cultural critique. Either way, we always notice how popular culture shows up in our participants' brainstorm ideas and in the stories they generate. If we feel that the popular culture example that is being mentioned may not be familiar to other participants, we make sure that we create a moment to introduce the general contours of that particular content world to everyone so it can be part of the conversation.

**Stories Matter.** The characters, conflicts and plot twists that the participants come up with during the course of the workshop are significant. In our workshops in the United States, superhero characters, entrepreneurs and political figures often make an appearance, as do corporations behaving for or against the public good. Outside the United States, we see many more instances of collective action (an instance where a village acts together), scientists, and institutions leading change. Often a natural or human-made crisis becomes a mobilizing event for change to take place.

**Watch for models of change.** Imaginations of how change could and should happen are implicit to the stories participants tell. Sometimes, an invention shared with a general public starts a process of change. Other times, the dedication of a few individuals who are able to tap their networks saves the day. In every instance, how participants see change happening point to the limitations and possibilities they perceive in their own communities. In some instances, participants even turn to magical processes to make change happen. We have found these moments particularly salient as they signal moments where our real world options seem inadequate, and magic becomes a necessary resort.

## Imagined Outcomes

In closing, we return to the Imagine 2040 event at the University of Southern California in 2017. On our return from lunch that day we organized the afternoon based on The World Cafe model of discussion and summarized it a blog write up following the event.

Civic Paths research assistants Samantha Close, Raffi Sarkissian and Yomna Elsayed each led a discussion to think through the outcomes that we could connect to the civic imagination. Overall, there was a strong sense that imagination could help some communities access a space of freedom and limitlessness simply to heal, to nurture and strengthen themselves. The tools and processes of civic imagination are not necessarily positive in and of themselves, and some of the educators described concerns they felt when working with college-aged students and realizing that they simply did not have a world view in which they saw themselves as civic actors with the potential to get involved.

Many dominant media narratives do not make enough room for diverse voices, visions and aspirations for justice and empowerment. The participants perceived a need for storytellers to push those boundaries outward, and for activists already engaged in those struggles to likewise connect that work with narratives and creative visions that could bring the stories of collective progress to the lives and imaginations of more people.

Actively practicing the civic imagination is a powerful way to enhance all kinds of action, from activism and organizing, to work done by creative professions and educators. The chronicles and workshops in this book support practitioners who want to add an imaginative dimension to their community facing work. Our vision is somewhat aspirational as it is really up to the readers and the growing community around the civic imagination to activate the materials we share. The imagination may enrich civic action as people think deeply about the narratives that motivate them. Our workshops can help groups form deeper connections with each other across divisions. The stories could grow and be put into action. The ideas generated can be nurtured to become robust media campaign ideas. But it's up to you to test those thoughts and imagine with us.

# Bibliography

Cechanowicz, Laura, Brian Cantrell, and Alex McDowell. 2016. "Worldbuilding and the Future of Media: A Case Study-Makoko 2036." *IEEE Technology and Society Magazine* 35(4) (December): 28–38.

Cohen, Cathy J. and Joseph Kahne. 2012. "Participatory Politics: New Media and Youth Political Action." MacArthur Foundation Youth and Participatory Politics Research Network (June). https://ypp.dmlcentral.net/publications/107.html

Dewey, John. 1934. *Art as Experience*. New York: Minton, Balch.

Duncombe, Stephen. 2012. "Utopia is No Place" Open Field: Conversations on the Common (in conversation with Sarah Peters). August 27. https://walkerart.org/magazine/stephen-duncombe-utopia-open-field

Forker, Charles. 1985. "The Green World Underworld of Early Shakespearean Tragedy" Shakespearean Studies: An Annual Gathering of Research. *Criticism and Review* 27.

Frye, Northrop. 1957. *Anatomy of Criticism: Four Essays by Northrop Frye*. Princeton: Princeton University Press.

Freire, Paulo. 2000. *Pedagogy of the Oppressed*. New York: Continuum.

Greene, Maxine. 1995. *Releasing the Imagination: Essays on Education, the Arts, and Social Change*. San Francisco: Jossey Bass.

Havel, Václav. 1990. *Disturbing the Peace: A Conversation with Karel Hvížďala* (Paul Wilson, Trans.) New York: Alfred A. Knopf.

Jenkins, Henry, Gabriel Peters-Lazaro, and Sangita Shresthova. 2020. *Popular Culture and the Civic Imagination: Case Studies of Creative Social Change*. New York: NYU Press.

Jenkins, Henry, Sangita Shresthova, Liana Gamber-Thompson, Neta Kligler-Vilenchik, and Arely M. Zimmerman. 2016. *By Any Media Necessary: The New Youth Activism*. New York: New York University Press.

# PRACTICE CHRONICLES

This section of the *Handbook* recounts how we developed our approach to the civic imagination. A series of community engagements stretching back to 2013 honed our workshop toolkit. We learned that every community context is unique and that successful creative collaborations require careful listening, diligent research and preparation, and a real openness to surprising discoveries within even the most familiar activities. Even in cases where we ran and re-ran the same basic workshop structures again and again, our learning outcomes and creative discoveries varied in profound ways. We share these recollections so the curious practitioner can understand our process and the learning we did along the way. Our process journey offers valuable lessons and perspectives to anyone hoping to bring civic imagination into their own communities, whether they will be working with familiar people or bringing that practice into new and unfamiliar contexts. Each chronicle includes a key learnings section that summarizes why this particular community engagement was important to developing the civic imagination approach and workshops.

The other thing we learned and demonstrate here, is that for all the variability and diversity we experienced taking these workshops around the world, the underlying human principles of caring and creativity are universal. As much as possible, we included details, not only about the specific backgrounds and contexts of the people and organizations we worked with, but also about the stories they made and the insights they shared. There are some wild imaginings contained herein, from improbable pop-culture mashups to touching visions of hope. In every case you'll read about people making a sincere effort to come together to share, explore and expand their visions and values as they helped us along our way to creating the workshop instructions that we detail in Section Three: The Practice Guidebook.

# CHAPTER TWO

# Fantasy Can Help Us Breathe—Muslim Youth Group, Los Angeles

## Key Insights

Working with the American Muslim Youth Group (MYG) confirmed that imagining and fantasy are important to our civic lives. In 2013, MYG reached out to us about running a workshop for their summer Leadership Program. These youth were under constant pressure to represent, even defend, Islam to the people in their lives. Inviting them to imagine and dream about the future freed them and allowed them to then return to their lives with a new appreciation for their, own and collective, agency. This experience also taught us that deploying the civic imagination in community contexts has to be porous enough to accommodate a change mid-stream. In this case, we retooled the workshop to encourage fantasy. We also had to trust that the civic and political would surface eventually. Through this, we gave the youth much *needed* permission to break out of their fraught and politicized identities as American Muslims and let their imagination roam.

## Introduction

Our journey into developing creative workshops began in 2013. The analysis phase of our multi-year research on youth, popular culture, and civic engagement had yielded insights into how young people were connecting cultural and political engagement, embracing new media affordances, and mobilizing communities around issues of concern. While sharing our findings through traditional academic channels was important to us, we felt there were additional opportunities to connect these insights to tools and practices that could be helpful to a broader audience, especially when it came to civic imagination. We wanted more communities to activate their collective imaginations in service of real world goals. To make this happen, we expanded our team at USC's Annenberg School of Communication and Journalism to include members from the School of Cinematic Arts with expertise in creating media rich learning experiences for youth. We also put the word out to educators and community leaders in our network, seeking partnerships to build materials for an iterative, creative, and collaborative process.

We leapt at the opportunity when the American Muslim Youth Group (MYG) reached out to us to develop and pilot a workshop at their summer Leadership Program in 2013. MYG is located at the Islamic Center of Southern California (ICSC), a mosque which sits near the heart of Los Angeles, just off Wilshire Boulevard. Unlike many mosques, ICSC does not formally align with any particular ethnic or sectarian group, though it was founded by Egyptian immigrants in the 1970s. In its activities, ICSC strives to engage diverse Muslim communities through an articulated belief (on their website) that the "values and principles found in the U.S. Constitution are in alignment with the eternal message of the Holy Quran."

We knew piloting work with MYG would present some distinct advantages and challenges. Challenges included the fact that we would be working with youth representing a broad range of ages from 5 to 14 years old. Also, due to safety concerns, we were not able to incorporate any field trips or excursions; all activities would be limited to ICSC premises. On the other hand, we would be able to work with the youth 2 hours every day for an entire week, which was an opportunity for deep engagement and creative collaboration. Another benefit of the partnership was that we would be working closely with a collective of young American Muslim artists called "Elev8." An Elev8 member served as a coordinator for the MYG program that summer and became one of our key collaborators.

## Post 9/11 Generation

We first connected with MYG a year earlier through our research on American Muslim youth, media and civic engagement. For that case study, Sangita Shresthova attended MYG's weekly Sunday school and interviewed youth who attended. This sustained engagement allowed us to build trust with the youth and program leadership. Summarized in the "Between Surveillance and Storytelling" chapter of the *By Any Media Necessary* (2016) book, this research explored participatory storytelling as a crucial form of civic expression and connection among American Muslim youth who had grown up in the decade following 9/11. Our findings informed how we approached piloting the workshops in 2013, so it is worth summarizing them briefly here.

Echoing the work of Sunaina Marr Maira (author of *The 9/11 Generation*, 2016) and other researchers (Genevieve Abdo, Nadine Naber, Amaney Jamal and others) working in this space, Shresthova's work confirmed the emergence of a "post 9/11 Generation" of youth who became civically engaged to protect the civil liberties of American Muslim youth. Though not new, anti-Muslim rhetoric and attacks on civil liberties experienced by American Muslims definitely increased after 9/11. Encouraged by this reality a new generation of activists and networks emerged. Aliyah, a young activist Shresthova interviewed during her research and cited in the "Between Storytelling and Surveillance" chapter of *By Any Media Necessary* (2016, online), summarized this experience when she observed:

> So, you're kind of still seeing that generation and the generations following it like pursuing the code of activism and civic engagement .... There were definitely people that were active before that but as a whole, the community was very insular. I'm in a great community trying to like get its feet on the ground, getting money, all that stuff, stability ... [After 9/11] I feel like that's when our community realized like, "Hold on. We need to get active. We need to do things because if not, we're screwed.

In introducing her ethnographic study of American Muslim youth, *The 9/11 Generation* (2016, 10), Sunaina Marr Maira confirms that a "shift in leadership occurred after 9/11" as younger second and third generation youth moved into leadership roles in American Muslim civic organizations that had previously been led by more recent immigrants. Maira is also quick to point out that getting civically active in no way protected these youths from being viewed with suspicion by the authorities who saw them as being at risk of "radicalization" (10).

This post 9/11 reality constituted the world in which the youth of MYG grew up. For them, MYG was a safe place where they could work through the issues they faced in their lives as they negotiated their American Muslim identities. Islam, citizenship, and civil liberties dominated their discussions. Some youth shared instances of ethnically motivated bullying. Others felt they needed to represent Islam and Muslims to their non-Muslim classmates, friends and broader communities, and felt ill equipped to defend a religion they were only starting to grasp themselves. Reflecting the civic imperative articulated by Aliyah, they also felt pressured to engage civically in claiming a future for American Muslims in the United States, which was often the only home they had ever known.

Between 2012 and 2013, MYG's activities included games, discussions, debates and close readings of the Qu'ran on themes relevant to youth, like music and even dating. Soha Yassine, the MYG coordinator at that time, saw civic engagement as an integral part of Islam. This theme was echoed by many of the guests she invited to address the youth, including controversial activist Malcolm Shabazz, grandson of Malcolm X. Questions of civil rights citizenship, race, and religion defined that particular session, which was also attended by other Nation of Islam members. The youth also often used MYG sessions to participate in American Muslim activist campaigns of the time such as the "My Jihad" project that sought to reclaim the original meaning of the term as a struggle for personal betterment. They also created the "Breakfast at Night" project inspired by "30Mosques," a campaign that collected stories of breaking fast during Ramadan.

## Fantasy Creeps In

In 2013, the summer Leadership Program represented a concerted effort by MYG to help the group be civically engaged within their communities. Our team had been developing a collaborative storytelling workshop based on the idea of world-building, and we agreed with MYG leadership that this would be a great framework for summer collaboration. The central idea of the worldbuilding work was to start with a freewheeling group brainstorm where we would collectively imagine and define a future world where anything was possible. This approach was informed by our team members' previous work with Alex McDowell and his World Building Institute. Beyond being a fun and engaging approach to creativity, worldbuilding presents a unique methodology for creative collaboration; it is non-hierarchical and nonlinear. Large groups of people can all agree to the broad characteristics that outline and define an imagined world, then work on their own individual or small group contributions by fleshing out stories that highlight particular aspects of that world. In this way, the resulting work can be both individual and collective. We thought this was a great fit with the MYG group and with our larger ambitions for creative engagements with activist and learning communities.

As much as we were excited to begin this work with MYG, we were concerned about needing to infuse the creative activities with civic and political concerns. We were afraid that if we only emphasized and facilitated creative and imaginative work with the group, we would not satisfy the (assumed) expectations of 'serious' work. So, we began with an agreed-upon approach that would be experimental and flexible, preserving an ability to react and adapt along with the leaders of the summer program. We knew that our worldbuilding activity at the beginning would serve as a launching point for a week-long engagement that would include instruction in media production. We thought that this second production phase would revolve around the participants finding their civic voice as young American Muslims, even though we weren't yet sure how that would play out.

On June 24, we ran our first ever future world brainstorm with the 21 youth participants at the MYG summer Leadership Program. We asked the youth to envision the year 2055 and a future world where anything was possible. We organized the brainstorm by riffing on several categories that would describe what this future world was like, including education, transport, and government. We expected that because of our setting at MYG and the ongoing discussions of civic engagement and Muslim identity, that the youth would reflect those discussions and ideas directly in their future visions. But we did not make this expectation explicit, and we certainly did not frame it as a requirement for the brainstorm. As youth came up with ideas for each of these categories for the world of 2055, we were struck by how quickly fantasy crept into the process. Soon, we were envisioning a world of rainbow grass, transportation bubbles, lions who spit knowledge, and flying carpets that made transportation limitations a thing of the past. The ideas got more and more creative and veered further and further away from our expectations of a literal vision of the future for Muslims and Islam in America. We spent the rest of that first session covering some basic video production skills. Once we wrapped up for the afternoon, we did a group huddle and reflected on how things had gone, and how to proceed.

At first, we attributed the turn toward the fantastical to the age of the participants; after all, aren't young people supposed to be the keepers of our ability to imagine? We also felt that as the workshop leaders, our next job would be to channel that fantastic outburst into more prosaic applications connected with civic engagement and issues facing the Muslim community. The artist and summer coordinator of the program offered an alternative interpretation and pathway forward. She observed that we had inadvertently given the youth much *needed* permission to break out of their fraught and politicized identities as American Muslims. To her mind, every day of these young people's lives was infused with the politicization of their identity; there was no need to frame their creative practices and experimentations in political or civic terms because they were already living that reality all the time. In other words, what they really needed was a space and framework in which to let their imaginations soar and play.

Our assumptions around the need to focus on the experiences of being young and American Muslim had almost made us stumble into perpetuating the very same politicization of identity that we had sought to counter through our workshop! These young people were tired. They were tired of always representing Islam among their peers. They were tired of always having their Muslim identity foregrounded. They wanted to do something different. They just wanted to let their imaginations roam without worrying about the political repercussions. Put bluntly, the youth needed fantasy to be able to breathe, connect, and exist beyond the politicized tensions that already defined their everyday lives.

## This Is Your Daily Fantasy Newscast: Up-ending Stereotypes

The coordinator's observation empowered us to fully embrace what had honestly been of more interest to us as a team in the first place—centering imagination and letting civics and politics emerge organically from that, if at all. We weren't exactly sure where this would lead, but since we felt that free-wheeling imagination was a benefit and boon in and of itself, we decided to trust the creative process. This approach would eventually lead to the central tenets of our process that would bear out in virtually all of our subsequent creative workshops in the following years; when you start with creativity and imagination, you don't abandon the real problems facing individuals, communities and the world, rather you learn to approach and see them in brand new ways, opening up possibilities for brand new solutions.

But on day one, we didn't know all that yet. To move forward with the task at hand, we radically expanded the scope of storytelling possibilities. On day two, we announced that we would all collectively produce stories that would all contribute to a future newscast for a day in 2055. We intentionally left out any mention of Islam or American Muslims. Instead, we invited the youth to form small groups and asked them to create a story that would elaborate on one element of our shared future world brainstorm from the day before. We felt that the newscast conceit was an elegant way of stitching these various stories together and also provided familiar genre and structural elements that would help shape and guide the translation of stories into actionable video projects.

The next three days were devoted to fleshing out their stories, creating simple storyboards visualizing their actions, using video cameras and tripods to capture their stories, and then using iMovie on Apple laptops to edit and shape their final contributions. While most of the groups were working out narrative stories, a separate group made up of the older participants in the group served as the anchor team. It was their task to create the framing elements of the newscast that would setup the world and tie together each of the narrative contributions, structuring them as reporting segments from the field. The whole package was called the "Daily Fantasy Newscast" and turned out to be a rich and colorful creative project.

The first news story featured mysterious babies falling from the sky, and included a live action scene with women excited to discover babies had rained on their car. The skit also featured an expert who pointed to a historical precedent for this phenomenon dating back to World War I. Unexpectedly, the babies then exploded.

The next report featured players competing in Marshmallow Bombs, a game developed by Immersion Inc., a video game company that supported collaboration between players. The winner (Billie Bob Joe) got to take home a game sword as a prize. The weather segment was interrupted when a Transformer hit a pedestrian. Luckily Ironman, who saw his heroic act as "all in a day's work," was nearby to lend a saving hand. A breaking news announcement cut to a press conference, where the president announced that the cows had been brought home from the moon, and that the crisis caused by their absence had been alleviated. "And that's it for today. Good morning, America!", was the cheery farewell that ended the newscast.

## Imaginary Bombs Are Off Limits

On the final day of the workshop, we all gathered to watch the final newscast as a group. Our initial screening was punctuated by giggles as the youth relished seeing their creations on the big screen.

As we (re)watched it, the mood in the room turned more serious as one participant observed that Muslims couldn't use bombs and explosions in their creative projects because of the ways in which it could be interpreted by the general public. The young women who had created that specific story were surprised by the comment, as it was not something they had considered as they had been swept up during their creative process. The explosion had simply fit within their story line.

At this point, the group coordinator led the group in a very engaged discussion about balancing creativity with audience; expression with reception. Did the participants, as American Muslims, have to bear the burden of representing their faith at all times? Did they need to protect their freedom to imagine, to escape this burden at times? When could they do this and how? The realities that we had bracketed at the beginning of the workshop had now re-entered the room as a complement, not a replacement to the fantastical imagination that we had nurtured through the past days.

Reflecting back on the week as our final day together drew to a close, one of the young people remarked that the fantasy we had created together had allowed them to just be themselves, even for a short time. We also realized that this short time could have a longer-lasting transformative effect. The MYG experience was formative for our work on the civic imagination as it gave us the confidence to lean more explicitly into foregrounding imagining as a needed process in our civic lives.

## Bibliography

Abdo, Genevieve. 2006. *Mecca and Mainstreet: Muslim Life in America After 9/11*. Oxford: Oxford University Press.

Gillum, Rachel M. 2018. *Muslims in a Post-9/11 America: A Survey of Attitudes and Beliefs and Their Implications for U.S. National Security Policy*. Michigan: University of Michigan Press.

Jamal, Amaney A. 2012. *Of Empires and Citizens: Pro-American Democracy or No Democracy at All?* Princeton: Princeton University Press.

Maira, Sunaina Marr. 2016. *The 9/11 Generation: Youth, Rights, Solidarity and the War on Terror*. New York: NYU Press.

Naber, Nadine. 2012. *Arab America: Gender, Cultural Politics, and Activism*. New York: NYU Press.

Shresthova, Sangita. 2016. "Between Storytelling and Surveillance: The Precarious Public of American Muslim Youth". In *By Any Media Necessary: The New Youth Activism*, eds. Henry Jenkins, Sangita Shresthova, Liana Gamber-Thompson, Neta Kligler-Vilenchik, and Arely M. Zimmerman. New York: NYU Press.

# CHAPTER THREE

# Bringing Imagination to Activism—Freedom School, Los Angeles

## KEY INSIGHTS

In the summers of 2013 and 2014, we worked with a Los Angeles site of the California Children's Defense Fund Freedom Schools program to run a week-long workshop on civic imagination, worldbuilding, and video making. Though they were congenial, our initial conversations with the organizers at the Freedom School involved a certain tension around our participation as outsiders. It soon became clear our creative interventions needed to complement community building and activist training taking place. Building trust over time, we created opportunities for young people to flex their creative muscles in playful ways that did not trivialize the importance of their activism. Working with these activists in training helped us articulate how the imagination can help issue-based struggles, strengthen group solidarity, and encourage future alliances.

## Introduction

"Is bringing the imagination to activism really a priority?" Over the course of our work on the civic imagination, we encountered this question often. Usually, it was asked by seasoned activists and social justice advocates committed to mobilizing around key social issues that confronted them and their communities; these issues were often directly connected with addressing basic needs and protecting lives. Their initial hesitation arose from an anxiety about "diverting" any energy and resources away from tackling those immediate problems and threats, and was, therefore, eminently understandable. These concerns mirrored many of our own initial thoughts when collaborating with the Muslim Youth Group and our original idea that imagination and creative engagements had to be somehow "justified" by their eventual turn back towards the practical and immediate civic or political concerns of the community.

Over time, we got better at articulating a response as we pointed out that the issue-focused work was precisely the reason why the civic imagination could be useful to these individuals and communities. For one, civic imagination workshops provide activists an opportunity to pause and think more broadly for a moment, which could encourage participants to re-frame their approach to social action. In his previously mentioned work on popular culture and political activism, Stephen Duncombe (Utopia is No Place, 2012 online) talks about the "tyranny of the possible" as a concept to describe the ways we get boxed in by our problem-based focus on immediate reality and concerns, and how useful it can be to seek ways out of such ruts. This concept has resonated with our experiences.

Our workshops also encourage participants to make connections to other topics and social issues, to think more about the long-term alliances and strategies they pursue. The workshops helped civically active participants stop for a minute and release some built-up tension as they connected with other participants. In other words, the workshops created a temporal and physical space that allowed participants to take a step back, take a breath, and then to return to the issues at hand with a refreshed, and slightly altered perspective. But, we had to discover and recognize all of this one workshop, one community, one story at a time. We also still have much more to learn about the transformational potential of the civic imagination.

In 2013 and 2014 we made great strides when we brought extended versions of our world-building workshops to the Los Angeles site of the California Children's Defense Fund (CDF) Freedom Schools. Rooted in the 1964 Mississippi Freedom summer and the Civil Rights Movement more broadly, the "CDF Freedom Schools" model seeks to "empower youth to excel and believe in their ability to make a difference in themselves, their families, communities, country and world with hope, education and action." (CDF Schools website). This core tenet was well aligned with our emergent understanding of civic imagination and learning to imagine oneself as a civic agent. Working through partnerships with schools and community organizations, the CDF Schools work bring free civically focused training to youth who may otherwise not have access to such programs.

# Building Trust with DREAM Activists

Our work with the CDF School in Los Angeles forced us to negotiate a certain tension around our participation as outsiders who did not define themselves in activist terms. Over the course of two consecutive summers we worked to build trust with the Freedom School organizers and participants. We worked hard to ensure that these experiences did not trivialize the importance of their work and the issues they grappled with. Rather, we sought to expand perspectives, include and amplify voices from within the community that were otherwise less present in group contexts, and to have fun while doing so.

The young people we worked with at the Freedom Schools were first and foremost engaged with the concerns of immigrant communities and especially with undocumented Latinx families. For this reason there was a clear link between this community and communities that Arely Zimmerman, a member of our team at the time, had worked with during earlier phases of the Media Activism and Participatory Politics Project around the DREAMers movement. The DREAMer movement advocated for immigration reform to support undocumented youth who had arrived in the United States as minors. Carried out between 2010 and 2011 with youth residing in California, Illinois, Georgia, and Texas, Zimmerman's qualitative study ("Documenting Dreams: New Media, Undocumented Youth and Immigrant Rights Movement 2012, 2) highlighted how youth involved with the movement had utilized new media to organize despite their "legal vulnerability." Her work also described how the circulation of such media supported and strengthened the communities and networks involved in these issues.

Zimmerman conducted her case study just as a revised version of the DREAM Act, or "bipartisan legislation that would provide an opportunity for undocumented students with 'good moral character' who have lived in the U.S. for a certain period, to obtain legal Status," (7) was being debated in the United States Congress. She focused on the in-person and online mobilization carried out by youth under the "undocumented and unafraid" slogan, which had included sit-ins at Congressional offices, hunger strikes, marches, symbolic graduations, and use of social media (10). Zimmerman's analysis also drew our attention to how the youth involved in the movement were able to tap 'participatory storytelling' (39) to link activism and storytelling in a new media environment:

> Sharing stories through various social and digital media platforms has allowed youth to challenge and, at times, supplant mass media representations through more locally constructed and participatory forms of messaging. Undocumented youth who engage in 'participatory storytelling' take advantage of new forms of social and digital media, along with their low barriers for participation, to come out as undocumented while

simultaneously reframing the immigrant rights debate through their personal narratives. This storytelling is not limited to oral testimonies or text, but is also circulated through movement art and user generated videos and documentaries, which present 'coming out' stories of undocumented youth. Sharing one's story involves high risk, and thus also fosters an ethos of trust, mutuality, and reciprocity that contributes to a sense of collective identification both in online and offline publics. (39)

Storytelling connects Zimmerman's work to Francesca Polletta, a social movement scholar, who contends that storytelling can help activists challenge policy centered framing that limits options around social issues. Though it is a common practice, storytelling remains somewhat underexplored, particularly in scholarly work on social movements. When addressed, storytelling is often subsumed within what Robert D. Benford and David A. Snow (2000, 614) call "framing", a directed approach that activates experiences towards targeted action. As Poletta notes, framing is specific and goal oriented. By contrast, storytelling thrives when it is allowed to be multifaceted and poignantly ambiguous.

## Building on 'Coming Out' Narratives

In her study, Zimmerman stressed the utility and impact of first person fictional storytelling. She observed that young people used the "coming out as undocumented" trope to gain visibility and connect with each other. She also noted that tapping popular culture narratives, like the ubiquitously familiar story of Superman, made their situation more understandable to others. After all, Superman was also an undocumented (albeit intergalactic) immigrant, who became a symbol of American values and justice! By adapting such narratives, DREAMers not only made their situation more relatable, they also infused it with the imaginative spark of a classic superhero story.

In 2013, we brought these insights to the Freedom School as we helped the youth create a future world newscast, just as we did with the Muslim Youth Group. The Freedom School participants were all high school-aged youth working with college-aged activist facilitators. They were immersed in the history of activism and struggles for civil rights in the United States. So, it was no surprise that the stories the youth created were very much about social justice and about marginalized communities overcoming political oppression and corporate exploitation.

In fact, the "Freedom School Network—The First on the Scene" newscast created by the youth opened with the news that in 2038, the "government has been overthrown" and elections were taking place. In a short skit, reporter Wendy White interviewed the two candidates running to replace the deposed president. The first (later successful) candidate believed that "we should not be classified by low class and high class". Her (losing) opponent believed that people have to work harder and pay for school.

Sticking to politically charged themes, the newscast then cut back to the youth created news studio, where an anchor shared some "not so happy news" of a "mother and two children who had been asked to leave the country". Through a short interview, the mother (who just so happened to be a unicorn), lamented that her family had been attacked on the street. Back in the studio, again, an immigration expert noted that, from an economic standpoint, immigration is not an issue. So "what would be a solution?" the anchors asked. "In the end, these are human beings, so we could house them," the expert responded.

The newscast continued. In another socially issue focused future news story, we learned that Apple had taken over the world and had raised its prices to unbearable levels. Protests were organized. Then came an unexpected, ad break, which featured a Gangnam Style inspired dance. As the newscast ended, we learned that in the world of 2038 everyone got to vote on the weather for tomorrow!

## Connecting Immigration, Protest and Unicorns

Drawing on their activist training, the participants were very clear about the stories they wanted to tell and the power dynamics they wanted to explore. They found ways to introduce key themes—like immigration and workers' rights—covered in their Freedom School curriculum into the stories they created. They also tapped activist centered approaches to accomplishing change—like protest and democratic participation. At the same time, they populated their stories with imaginary elements like unicorns and used the newscast format to introduce playful moments.

In terms of video production, we did our best to take a hands-off approach, to give them just the barest introduction to the tools and allow them to learn for themselves (with our support when questions came up), rather than giving them a top-down lesson in the 'right way to do things.' This approach is aligned with our own commitment to participatory media making; it was also consistent with the Freedom School's approach to supporting a sense of collective self-efficacy and agency.

Our approach was confirmed as we observed the participants creating their newscast story videos. As they worked together to figure out the details of how to create their storyboards, stage and film scenes, the youth connected with each other and pooled their collective skill sets to complete the task at hand. In this way, the practices of video production were a more direct extension of the creative and civic impetus from which they grew. The resulting media products then served as a basis for reflection, discussion and further creative and technical growth. Youth saw and shared their successes and mistakes, fueling a cycle of creative iteration and refinement as we maintained our role as mentors that was based on minimal intervention.

## Engaging Memory Objects

When we returned to the Freedom School the following summer, we added new components to the workshop including: the creation of artifacts from the students' stories, an engagement of memory objects, and a more explicit focus on building narratives set in a future world without borders.

Once again, we integrated our session within the Freedom School framework, which made use of temporal frames (past, present, future) that year. Notably, some of the activities the youth had carried out prior to our arrival directly connected to the civic imagination. For example, the youth had composed a collective poem that articulated their individual aspirations for the future. The poem included these verses:

> Imagine a world with no borders
> A place where you always feel you're at home
> Communities, friends and family will finally come together
> There are no races but human beings
> We are all family
> They are imaginary square root of -1
> The limits live in me & I have already crossed them
> Keep Going
> History changes dramatically
> Families wouldn't be separate
> I get to go everywhere
> We will all be equal and free …..

The Freedom School facilitators had also posted a timeline documenting key moments in the history of immigration related violence, discrimination and reform in the United States in the space. These included more historical events like the 1492 "Genocide of indigenous people begins with Christopher Columbus voyage to the Americas" and the 1830 Removal Act which Forced 70,000 Native Americans to relocate in order to free land for European immigrants as well as more contemporary events like the passing of the California DREAM Act in 2011 and President Obama's Deferred Action for Childhood Arrivals (DACA) executive order of 2012. The youth had then used colorful post-its to add their own personal memories to the timeline. These featured statements like "Mom came to US" (1983) and "My birthday—December 29, 1999".

When we saw the poem and the timeline, we decided to use them to anchor our world-building exercise to the Freedom School curriculum. Laying down the foundation for what later became the Origin Stories workshop, we developed an icebreaker that played with objects and memory as we asked each participant to share a memory of an object or artifact they had once owned but that they had since lost. Painful, incredibly poignant, accounts of memories, loss and human connection emerged as we went around the room. One youth shared that he remembered a bag of marbles that had always played with as a small child. He forgot to take them with him when he left for the US with his parents. He had no idea what had happened to them, and connected them to a carefree childhood he left behind, as he had never been able to return to his home in Mexico. One of the youth leaders shared the story of a VHS tape recording of her and her best friend she brought with her when she immigrated as a child to the United States. The tape was the only tangible connection she had to her friend, and one day she returned home from school to discover that her mother had accidentally recorded a telenovela over the recording. As she described the moment when she realized the recording of her friend was gone forever, the young woman's voice broke with emotion.

Building on this foundation of memory, artifacts and how our own narratives connect to larger world events, we led the future world brainstorm focused on envisioning a world without borders in 2044. We "extended" the immigration timeline and worked backwards with the youth to identify key moments that could occur between 2014 and 2044:

2020 – worldwide health care provided
2026 – conflict that ends racism
2032 – super brains bring about technological leap
2038 – world government and language
2044 – wars banned

The youth then worked in smaller groups to create stories connected to those key events. They created artifacts from those stories that could serve as memory objects from the future. These artifacts took the shape of short videos, a 'hover car' made out of cardboard, and sign featuring a protest slogan.

## Accommodating Utopias and Dystopias in Activism

Much like the year before, the stories the Freedom School youth created connected to the social issues that were relevant to the youth's lives. They also revealed a multifaceted and at times complicated, even conflicted, future world. For example, the story created by the year 2020 group focused on an immigrant woman named Maria who got injured while working in a hotel. As she "didn't have papers", she couldn't access health care for her injury. Through a conversation with a co-worker, she learned about the recent passing of the global Health Act and realized she could access care, even if she was not a citizen of the United States. The 2026 group shared a story that began with the realization that the passing of the Global Health Act had not ended racism. In fact, some countries, specifically European countries, were able "to get access to better care, better hospitals, better doctors because those countries had better resources". Once they discovered this, leaders of African countries started a media campaign to increase awareness of this issue and start a movement to end such (racial) discrimination. Other developing countries soon joined the movement, leading to changed policy and a "domino effect", whereby access to better care led to a "leveling of the playing field" in terms of education and access to employment.

Working our way through such key, but never fully resolved, future moments, we reached 2044 when all wars have been banned because a benevolent dictator has come to power. To guarantee universal happiness, he also issued an order for a compulsory "happiness" vaccine that must be administered to everyone, assuring they are always happy. We learned of a young woman who tried to resist, but is eventually forcefully injected with the serum, in a (dubious) assurance of universal happiness as the end state of the world in 2044.

As we reflected on our Freedom School experiences, we noted key elements that helped us find ways to connect our approach to the civic imagination to their social justice and activist goals over the two years of our involvement. Though initially counter-intuitive, our decision to focus on process, rather than outcome, allowed us to use the workshop as a space for exploration and playfulness. The integration of memory objects allowed us to build in an approach that stressed affective connection from the beginning. Our participation in this moment in the workshop also helped us establish trust. Through we have since sometimes omitted its use, the use of a timeline as a bridge between larger historical events and more personal ones helped situate the civic imagination as an extension of the past and present in ways that facilitated a connection between our approach and that of the Freedom School. Building physical artifacts and stressing the live performance component of the workshop further helped us connect the real and the imagined. And finally, we recognized that the utopian impulse to imagine an aspirational future world can just as importantly surface more dystopian visions. Like a future world where happiness is forcefully guaranteed by a benevolent dictator, such dystopias can push participants to think deeply about their understanding of the continuing negotiations involved in advocating for social change. Drawing out these elements, helped us bring imagination to the young people learning to see themselves as agents of change as they trained in the skills and practices of activism. The experience also helped us advocate imagination and playful creativity within a spaces intentionally crafted for political action.

## Bibliography

Benford, Robert D. and David A. Snow. 2000. "Framing Processes and Social Movements: An Overview and Assessment". *Annual Review of Sociology* 26: 611–639.

Duncombe, Stephen. 2012. "Utopia is No Place" Open Field: Conversations on the Common (in conversation with Sarah Peters). August 27. https://walkerart.org/magazine/stephen-duncombe-utopia-open-field

Polletta, Francesca. 2006. *It Was Like a Fever: Storytelling in Protest and Politics*. Chicago: University of Chicago Press.

Zimmerman, Arely. 2012. "Documenting Dreams: New Media, Undocumented Youth and Immigrant Rights Movement". *DML Research Hub*. https://dmlhub.net/publications/documenting-dreams-new-media-undocumented-youth-and-the-immigrant-rights-movement/

# Mind Blown! Grown Ups Freaking Out—Digital Media and Learning Conference, Boston

## KEY INSIGHTS

On March 7, 2014, we ran our worldbuilding workshop with 35 participants at the Digital Media and Learning Conference in Boston Massachusetts. The participants enthusiastically embraced our invitation to fantasize, confirming that the civic imagination has as much to offer adults as much as it does to youth and children. The participants were educators, academics, librarians, and community program coordinators who collectively highlighted how powerful the invitation to imagine and play can be, especially if they have few such opportunities. Coming out of the workshop, the participants enthusiastically advocated for practing a shared imagination as something they wanted and needed in their professional lives.

## Introduction

"No more school buildings!" is a demand we encountered often when we ran our workshops in educational settings. Though it might sound self destructive at first glance, this sentiment was actually representative of a generative energy that we often heard as part of a future world vision wherein learning would happen everywhere not just in designated settings, a world where the constraints of class periods and limited recess time would be things of the past. Visions of this sort were consistently articulated by educators and others involved with teaching and learning as they embraced our invitation to think outside of existing structures and dared to imagine a future filled with possibilities rather than just challenges.

As we think back, the adults we have encountered through our educator-facing work—including teachers, librarians and after-school program coordinators—have been among the most enthusiastic supporters of our brainstorms. They willingly accepted our invitation to fantasize and, in the words of one early participant, have their "minds blown." In this chapter, we revisit the first such workshop we ran with an all-adult education-oriented group. It was an important turning point for our team and the development of our approach as we tested the waters of "grown up" imagination.

On March 7, 2014, we ran our third worldbuilding workshop at the Digital Media and Learning (DML) Conference in Boston Massachusetts. Founded in 2011 and funded by the MacArthur Foundation, the DML conference brought together educators, academics and practitioners whose work engaged the intersection of education and digital media, broadly defined. Organized around panel discussions, shorter presentations, screenings, and plenaries, the conference helped support the emergence of a network that collectively contributed to developing "connected learning," a new approach that sought to connect "fragmented spheres of a young person's life—interests, academic and work opportunities, and peer culture" (MacArthur Foundation Digital Media and Learning website). While more relaxed than many traditional conferences, DML still relied on the basic conventions of conference going that foreground professional networking and sharing of best practices. Predictably, digital media was also a key element of the event, as tweeting and live streaming were generally encouraged in an effort to reach a broader, geographically removed, audience.

In our conference session application, we proposed to run a shortened version of the future world building workshops we had run that summer with the Muslim Youth Group (MYG) at the Islamic Center of Southern California and with the Children's Defense Fund's Freedom School in Los Angeles. Once our proposal was accepted, we worked with both the MYG group coordinator and the Freedom School coordinator, our community partners, to adapt our method to a conference setting. We carefully thought through the instructions and considered what elements of the workshop had worked well with young people and how these might translate to an adult only context. In the end, we made a conscious decision to make very few changes in the hopes that we could bring the sense of playfulness that had defined our work with youth to our session at DML. We decided to be explicit about how our summer sessions had strengthened our belief that our approach presented a much needed invitation to bring the imagination to civics. We also decided to share how much the young people in both of those locations had appreciated this as a moment of respite from their everyday lives and activities in the way that we introduced and framed the workshop at DML.

## Launching the Workshop

Walking into the room for our session at DML, we were shocked (and delighted) when we realized that 35 people had showed up for our session. We had thought we might only have 10 or 15 people. The participants were made up of educators, academics, librarians and community program coordinators. There was an air of anticipation in the room. We were nervous as we introduced ourselves and our team from USC. We then turned the floor over to the group coordinators who shared some initial thoughts about our continuing collaboration. The Freedom School coordinator, who participated via video-conferencing, talked about our shared commitment to participatory facilitation and how that allowed us to work effectively together:

> "The most important thing was that … our role was to be facilitators. The youth had a story to tell. They needed to find their voice, whatever that was. We weren't trying to teach anything, that was the most important thing to me. We were all hanging back. We were there for technical help and guidance, questions. But the students ran every piece of it and a lot of really good stuff came out of it."

The Muslim Youth Group coordinator shared her perspective on the youth at the Islamic Center of Southern California and why our work there had been so cathartic for everyone involved:

> "Part of what the work I have done with the Islamic Center youth for little over a decade now is using the arts and creativity… to create your own story, to document your own story. The thing that is relevant in terms of the Muslim American community is that is a community whose identity is largely shaped by the outside definitions of what it is to be Muslim. For us, working with our community in LA, the importance becomes how do you define identity in the first person and not become part of the self-fulfilling prophecy of being told what you are and being limited in terms of your imagination of what you are."

Taking a deep breath, we then moved forward with the workshop. We ran a quick icebreaker that invited participants to come up with a one word response to a key word prompt. Given the focus of the conference, our prompts included words like twitter, education, and home. We created a quick video to collate all the responses and played it back to all the participants as a way to start the workshop and lower perceived barriers to participation and creative expression. As everyone's face appeared on the screen and nervous laughter released some initial tension, we started to feel an initial sense of connection between participants.

Following our worldbuilding workshop flow, we then asked the participants to imagine a world in 2044, a world where borders would be a thing of the past. This led to an enthusiastic brainstorm that featured flying shoes, customizable nutrition, universal translators, clothes that talk, and brain mail. The participants then had a limited time to work in smaller groups to come up with stories to populate the world. This is when the room exploded with excitement as people started to brainstorm story ideas. As we walked around, we heard people sharing their favorite pop culture characters, enacting key moments in stories, and sharing their hopes and fears for the future.

When we announced the participants had a few minutes to translate their stories into impromptu performances that would be performed for the whole group, there was some hesitation. We noticed that some participants even eyed the door at that moment, but in the end no one left. Instead, they committed to making the performances happen with their groups.

## Educators Imagine the Future of Learning

The stories the participants shared confirmed our commitment to the imagination, and its applicability to both youth and adults. Here are some of them:

> **Story 1:** The year was 2014, and a group of researchers around the world began collaborating on language preservation and collecting data on every language known to earth [frantic typing and sample collecting gestures]. They started creating a prototype for an early version of a translator for all languages [hand puppet gestures]. Meanwhile, in 2015, Esperanza a high school student from earth lost family members in a devastating event due to language barriers and conflict. By 2016, the world was riddled with conflict caused by the loss of languages and resulting inability to communicate, many people were against these efforts. So researchers responded by starting to create prototypes to translate languages to implant directly into people's brains. This, in turn, animated resistance by anti-cyborg groups which caused funding sources to stall (protest sign waving gestures). In 2025, Esperanza came back to the public stage and she volunteered to be the first person to have the universal translator chip planted into her brain. She demonstrated that the procedure is safe and effective.

She became a known negotiator between these tribes in conflict and everyone lived happily ever after?

**Story 2:** It is the year 2014, and at the Digital Media Learning conference everyone and their brother, their mother, their sister, and their friends were on their devices trying to social network their lives away. Be-ing, an international travel student from Beijing was there trying to break in but she couldn't communicate what she was learning to everyone back home because of closed social networks. So Be-ing, having double majored in linguistics and fashion, decided this is a great opportunity to go on and get an education in computer science because everyone at DML knows everything about computers. We fast forward to the year 2020 and Be-ing has received her masters and Ph.D. in computer science and programming. She developed a brand new technology, Smart Fabric. Smart Fabric was packed with remix capabilities, was completely hackable and was available for all people. This, all of a sudden, allowed Be-Ing to communicate with everyone around her. So Be-Ing lived in a world where instead of using devices to communicate with the network, people just communicated and connected. There was a connection between the smart fabric and the chips already implanted in their heads. With the touch of a shoulder, Be-Ing could friend, Be-Ing could follow, and Be-Ing could post.

**Story 3:** The day was Saturday. It was the last day of the DML conference in 2014 and everybody was laughing and talking and sharing insights in their various languages. Suddenly aliens invaded and decided it was way too confusing to have all these languages and they made everyone speak in binary code. Thirty years later, one woman decided she wanted to preserve her language so she took her newborn daughter under her wing and secretly taught her their original tongue. But then, the mother was captured by the aliens and put in alien prison where she died. Her daughter traveled across the world trying to find speakers of the secret hidden language but people were very reluctant to admit it for fear that they would also go to alien prison. As she traveled the world, the daughter sought supporters who concealed her so the aliens wouldn't discover who she was that she had been secretly using her clothes, her body language and other signals. Then one day she went to the alien headquarters and there was a revolution—LASAGNA (holler) REVOLUTION (and response). Fists went up in the air. And everyone went back to speaking their various languages.

# Imagination as a Digital Citizenship Skill

As the applause subsided after the last performance, we all were moved by what we had just experienced and started to reflect on what had just happened. One participant noted that the story creation process was "tremendous fun" as her group members "were talking over one another and jumping up and down."

Another participant noted how inspired he was as the creativity was coming together. "It felt like we were all kids", he laughed and continued, "We were excited when we were coming up with another idea. Ooh yeah! It just hit us,… how impactful creativity can be, working with folks that you've never met."

Focusing on the performances, some participants noted that this was the hardest part of the workshop for them. Another participant defended our choice:

> I like to think about improvisational theater … as a place to practice skills for digital citizenship because you are learning through play, you are connecting, and listening. You are rapid prototyping and being sensitive about audience.

Quite surprisingly for the context of a conference on digital media, several participants shared how liberating it felt to put their devices aside and to connect with each other on an interpersonal level. One participant noted during the workshop, people weren't on their phones, they "were interacting with one another." This was echoed by another participant who felt this was a new experience for him within DML:

> This is my third year at this specific conference and for the first time in those three years … I am so used to this and I'm sure it's the same for those who have been here, it's like everyone is here and while we are interacting, everyone is tweeting away. For the first time, there is a sense of connectivity beyond the device.

Many of the educators and organizers in the room were already devising ways of bringing this activity to the youth "back home".

As he reflected on the totality of the workshop, Andrew Slack, the founder of Harry Potter Alliance who had worked with us on various projects in the past, observed that our workshop uses storytelling as a sort of boiling point where "all sorts of disciplines fuse":

> People tell their story through a once removed character, people reflecting on own story as a world, mythological stories—any one of these stories, you could do research— look at language and imperialism, history, identity, a lot happens in the boiling point. The educational opportunities are transcendent.

He then concluded that the workshop invites participants to get "to the political without sacrificing the right to pretend." Instead, we encourage the participants to get to the political "by amplifying the right to pretend."

The workshop ended with an enthusiastic round of applause and exclamations of support for the workshop. "Lasagna Revolution," the rallying cry from one of our sessions became a trending Twitter hashtag at the conference, a development that made the workshop a subject of discussion for the next few days.

The participants' experiences with this workshop highlighted how powerful the invitation to imagine and play can be for adults, especially if they have few such opportunities. In particular, the workshop pushed past the constraints of their everyday lives and connected them to other participants in playful ways that cut through the social barriers usually associated with conference setting encounters. This was a powerful affirmation for us. Creative energy and imagination can fuel community. We left the session motivated to translate and adapt our approach into other locales and contexts where bridge building and civic participation were needed.

# CHAPTER FIVE

# Em/power Love: Building Empathy and Solidarity with Each Other— Salzburg Global Seminar

## KEY INSIGHTS

Every year the Salzburg Academy on Media and Global Change brings students from around the world together for a three-week intensive practical and theoretical training. We piloted the Remixing Stories workshop with these students in 2016. Testing our approach, we asked them to share stories that mattered most in their lives. We then worked with them to migrate and remix their stories, to create completely new narratives emerging from creative dialogue. As their stories emerged and the students reflected on their experiences, we were struck by the power of their narratives and the potential for civic imagination to serve as a powerful catalyst for cross-cultural dialogue through creative exchange.

## Introduction

When interviewed, Sally[1] told us that our civic imagination workshop had allowed her to activate her imagination in ways that she was not often invited to do:

---

1. Name has been altered to protect identity of participant.

The whole idea of not being held back by what can be realistic. Interpreting all of these things in a creative way was really, really fun for me because we got to sit there and think of all these mad ideas and then construct something from there. I thought the creative aspect to get [to] a bigger message was a really cool thing.

As an undergraduate student in Journalism at Bournemouth University in the United Kingdom, she rarely had the opportunity to exercise her imagination. In fact, those opportunities had always been few and far between in her school life, where imagination was often relegated to art classes. She also appreciated that she got to share her imagination with others. She observed that storytelling had enabled her to share something very intimate with her team members, something that broke past her expectations of what could happen in a classroom setting. Sally shared these reflections in an interview that followed a civic imagination workshop series we ran at the Salzburg Academy for Media and Global Change in Austria in 2016. The academy is a college accredited summer program run by the Salzburg Global Seminar that brings together students from around the world for a three-week intensive training in media, storytelling, activism and social change.

That summer we made great progress in our work on the civic imagination as running our workshop with 80 students over several weeks allowed us to test, fine tune and expand on our approach. This expansion included the launch of a prototype tool allowing us to visually represent individual and collective visions generated through our workshop sessions. It was also the first time we ran what later became the Remixing Stories workshop.

We organized our workshops at the Academy around three sessions. In the first session, we introduced the civic imagination though a future worldbuilding exercise that invited the participants to envision the world of 2066. In the second session, we channeled the energy of the team into a more individually focused process of surfacing and sharing stories. In our final session we provided participants with an opportunity to explore each other's stories before they worked together to "migrate" them and create entirely new stories by combining elements of each of the sources. Throughout, we collected stories into a prototype website charting each contribution on a series of maps as a way to see their global spread. We named this archive the Atlas of the Civic Imagination, to signal towards the spatial dimensions of our collective storytelling process.

The transnational nature of the academy, with participants coming from as many as 30 different countries, led to rich creative explorations through stories from students' own lives and popular cultures that they believed contained inspirations for civic engagement. As expected, this allowed us to deepen our understanding of how the civic imagination could support dialogue across cultural and social differences. We were surprised when we discovered that the location of the

Academy itself had a lot to teach us about how the civic imagination manifests through history of place.

## Schloss Leopoldskron

The Schloss Leopoldskron (which locals refer to simply as the Schloss) is an 18th century lakeside palace in Salzburg, Austria. Entering through its gates, one is struck by the almost oppressive weight of its beauty. Passing through its grounds, ballrooms, and libraries feels very much like a walk into its rich and troubled past. The history of the Schloss includes Mozart, protestant suppression, Max Rheinhardt's creative experiments, the film The Sound of Music, the Third Reich and the seminal anthropology scholar, Margaret Mead. It has served as a home and stage to arts and artists, prince-archbishops and propagandists, soldiers and war criminals who imbued the place with competing imaginations of the present, past, and future.

Built in 1736, the Schloss was initially under the ownership of Prince-Archbishop of Salzburg Count Leopold Anton Eleutherius von Firmian and his extended family, who had orchestrated, and benefited from, the forceful removal of Protestants from the city. After the family's demise, the Schloss moved from owner to owner until theater and film director Max Reinhardt purchased it in 1918, two years before he went on to found the Salzburg Festival. Reinhardt undertook many renovations in the space as a labor of love and with the vision that the Schloss would become a cultural center and a place where creative people (artists, composers, thinkers) would gather. In Reinhardt's vision, the Schloss would support experimentation, frank exchange and creative expression. His tenure and activities at the Schloss were cut short when he, as a Jew, was forced to flee Austria when it became part of the German Third Reich through the "Anschluss" of 1938.

In 1939, the German government seized the Schloss as Jewish property and proceeded to assign it to party cronies who were encouraged to use it as a space where party elites could gather, socialize and enjoy life within proximity of the Obersalzberg region where many prominent Nazis, including Adolf Hitler, owned houses. In fact, Obersalzberg and the surrounding areas (including the Schloss itself) were very much part of the ideal imaginary, or what Horst Möller (2002) and his colleagues call the "tödliche Utopie" (fatal utopia) that the Nazis envisioned as a part of their terrifying post-Endlösung (final solution) new world order.

After the war, a slightly war-damaged Schloss became the home of the Salzburg Global Seminar (SGS), an organization that owes its existence to three Harvard graduate students who came to Austria in the aftermath of World War

II eager to create and implement a "Marshall Plan of the Mind." Early gatherings they organized at the Schloss included academic exchanges (focused initially on American Studies) and in-person meetings that brought together diverse participants in the hopes that there could be ways to encourage them to speak to each other. The aim was to support them as they connected, exchanged ideas, and ultimately helped rebuild Europe after World War II. Often cited as a key moment for the founding of the SGS, one of the early sessions hosted at the Schloss included both former members of the Nazi party and Holocaust survivors just a few years after the war had ended. A note taker of one such session moderated by seminal anthropologist Margaret Mead observed that the:

> Salzburg Seminar proved that the vertical partitions of nationality are not insuperable barriers in Europe today. The more permanent horizontal relationships—common interests, similar traits of mind, shared curiosity or confusion or enthusiasm, mere likeness and liking among individuals—these turned out to be available channels for the renewal of communication. (meeting notes 1948)

Since then, SGS had built on this legacy and vision of a more inclusive future built on exchange and has grown into a formal institution that encourages dialogue and collaboration through ongoing hosted events and on the ground programs in multiple locations around the world. SGS has also nurtured a reflective, even introspective identity in its effort to support exchanges across political and other divides that would otherwise not be possible. The very nature and existence of the Seminar and its location at the Schloss requires its visitors to think through their perception of and agency within the dynamic flows of time connecting past, present and future. The Academy is a program of SGS.

In 2016, the Academy took place in the immediate shadow of the Brexit vote and the unsettling approach of the U.S. presidential election. We were also in the midst of Europe's ongoing refugee crisis when more than 1 million new asylum applications were registered within the European Union in 2015. Responding to these real world events, the 2016 Academy addressed issues surrounding media and migration with the hope that the civic imagination could encourage the students to find new approaches to grappling with these unsettling issues. The Schloss's almost oppressive beauty, it's complicated history, and significant location in the heart of Austria weighed heavily on our consciousness as we guided the students towards imagining aspirational futures.

## Connecting to Others through the Inspiring Stories

To get the students warmed up to imaginative thinking, we started with a group future world-building exercise, which asked them to envision the world of 2066.

The students ran with this and soon a world where battles are relegated to outer space, women lead the world, teleportation is a telepathic action, and the world has been united by an apocalyptic depletion of natural resources began to establish a baseline of shared values and aspirations in the room.

We then asked Academy students to share stories that mattered most in their lives, that they felt could help bind communities in shared values and inspire action for positive social change. As soon as we introduced the topic, Tina a young woman of Nigerian origin who grew up in the United Kingdom, lit up, raised her hand and exclaimed, "I have a story to share!" She then reached into her past to share a story that her mother used to tell her when she was a little girl. This was the story of how the tortoise cracked its shell:

> Once upon a time, way before any man walked upon this earth, there was a great famine all throughout Africa. Many animals died, many animals who survived were starving badly. This included the tortoise, who grew skinnier and skinnier with each passing day. One day he was sitting outside his home when he looked up and saw the birds flying overhead. Unlike all the other animals in the land, they looked fat and well fed. Wondering why the birds were so fat and he was so thin, he called down a bird and asked him why he was so fat. The bird replied that he, along with all his brothers and sister, had a kind benefactor that lived in the clouds and gave them food to eat. Upon finding this out, tortoise begged the bird to take him with him the next time he went. Laughing, the bird asked how he, a small fat bird, would carry the big tortoise to the clouds. The tortoise, who was so smart, saw two sticks on the ground and explained to the tortoise that he would hold the stick in his mouth and the bird should hold the other end with his feet. By using his powerful wings, tortoise explained, the bird would be able to carry him. Initially the birds were fooled by the tortoise and accommodated him. But eventually, they realized that he was a liar and that he just wanted to just take away their food. So, they let him fall out of the sky, which is how he cracked his shell.

After she narrated the story to the whole group, Tina shared how the story inspired to "be truthful" and how it also reminded her to "see the funny side of life". She also explained how the story helped her feel connected to her Nigerian heritage and her mother's culture as she grew up in a 'predominantly white primary school'. As she concluded her story, many students in the session nodded, clearly moved by the story. Even though her narration had ended, Tina face continued to glow, her demeanor, and way of relating to her classmates, had completely changed.

Building on this example, we asked all of the students to look into their past to come up with their own meaningful stories. What they shared included folk tales, literary classics, contemporary popular media, national history and personal narratives. Stories contributed by students included the Disney feature film *Lion King*, which allowed a British student to connect to his African heritage and religious beliefs, and El Dorado, a legend that fueled European's insatiable hunger for gold in South America that reminded the contributor of the ebbs and flows of history.

Working in small groups, the students then shared these individual stories with each other. Through this, they learned about each other. They learned where they came from and what mattered to them. They learned what motivated them. They learned about the experiences they valued. We then asked them to add their individual stories to a shared google map that made all of the stories visible and navigable.

## Remixing Stories

Once the students shared their individual stories among themselves, we asked them to work in smaller groups to migrate and remix their stories, to create completely new narratives emerging from creative dialogue. We suggested that they employ several strategies for these story migrations, including but not limited to: moving a character from one story into another, creating a new character by combining aspects of several characters, adapting a key moment, event or theme from one story into another, or moving a story from one location to another.

After a moment of hesitation, their stories started to emerge. In one group, three young women joined forces to take elements from three very different stories that had been inspirational to them individually and created something completely new collectively. Their new story was called "Em/Power Love" and envisioned the main character (and author) of *Eat Pray Love*, Liz Gilbert, traveling to Brazil and falling in love with famed photographer Sebastiao Salgado. Together, Liz and Sebastiao travel through Brazil documenting injustice until a mysterious comet appears and delivers an extraterrestrial named Em (a character from the animated series *Sailor Moon*) in their midst. Em has come to warn the lovers that the universal council is about to agree to destroy Earth because of all the injustice being perpetrated between human beings. She reveals that the planet can only be saved if someone proves that it is worth preserving because there are many good things happening and that efforts are underway to address gender inequality. Rising to the occasion, Liz and Sebastiao work together with Em who uses her magical powers to help them travel the globe. Together, they document and photograph those fighting against gender-based injustice. They present a convincing case to the council and are able to save Earth from being destroyed.

Another group drew on *Chef*, a 2014 film focused on the art and love of cooking, and a real-world account of doctor volunteers who took to the Aegean sea to provide medical care to refugees crossing into Europe to create a narrative focused on migration to Europe triggered by the conflict in Syria. In this group's remixed story, a successful American chef learns about the refugee crisis in the Mediterranean through his Facebook account, he decides to look into the situation further. After some initial research, he reaches out to the Aegean doctor team. They invite him to join them and bring fresh, well cooked, food to the islands filled with stranded refugees. He agrees to travel with them. He shares his food with everyone he meets and collects migrants' stories along the way. Upon returning home, the chef shares the stories he collected with his audience, and through this changes how refugees are perceived by people who would have otherwise probably not learned about their plight.

These and other stories created through the workshop demonstrated how remixing individual stories offered the participants new ways to see each other, the world around them, and the values they shared. As one Syrian participant put it, "despite the fact that we come from different backgrounds, we all have the same values." As the students continued to reflect on their experiences with us, we were struck by the power of their narratives and the potential for civic imagination to serve as a powerful catalyst for relationship and network building.

The Remixing Workshop experience also seeded ideas for social action as some students built on the stories they had generated as they developed their final media campaign projects. For example, one of the students in the Chef of the Aegean story group created an interactive map to share stories of migration through food. His culinary project celebrated cooking food, mixing flavors, and substituting ingredients as a form of cross cultural dialogue. (MY)Gration, another project created by Academy students that year, used physical objects carried by migrants as they moved from one location to another as entry points into stories that bridged between the past and future. Yet another group developed a participatory storytelling project that tried to "flip the narrative" around migration by collecting positive (inspiring) accounts of how migration enriched receiving communities.

Seeing these, and other, narratives and projects come to life, confirmed that migrating stories could infuse our perceptions and conceptual frames around migration with an enhanced sense of the human creativity and imagination inherent within any individual and their community, both in terms of where they come from and where they are going. As we saw the stories coming in from the small working groups, and as we began to discuss the process of creating these new migrated stories, we saw an initial indication that at least at this micro level our intentions were playing out in a positive manner. Participants spoke of the initial challenges of finding common ground amongst their apparently very different stories, and that through negotiating the imaginative terms of a new narrative they each gained a deeper understanding not only of each other but of their own contributions and the values inherent within their choices.

## Towards a Lasting Connection and the Atlas of the Civic Imagination

Experimenting with a visual tool throughout the sessions allowed us to explore how the inspiring and remixed stories generated could be rendered visible to the participants and eventually to a broader general public as well. While the workshops described in this volume focus on applying our methodology to specific groups, collecting narratives to facilitate a thematic and geographical mapping has always been an integral to our vision of how the civic imagination can be activated and mobilized. To make this vision a reality we have since created a publicly usable Atlas of the Civic Imagination (www.ciatlas.org).

Just as the Schloss serves as a gathering place for contemplation of the past and future, building a depository—in the form of an Atlas—mapped our pathways toward a more inclusive and participatory approach to the civic imagination. By connecting otherwise disparate communities through a sharing of their aspirational worlds and space, the Atlas enables us to radically expand the scope of the civic imagination to embrace and transcend the pasts that define us in search of the futures that we can all build together.

## Bibliography

Möller, Horst. 2002. *Die Tödliche Utopie: Bilder, Texte, Dokumente, Daten zum Dritten Reich.* Munich: Institut für Zeitgeschichte.

# CHAPTER SIX

# Turning the Chairs to Face the Table—Bowling Green, Kentucky

## KEY INSIGHTS

In September 2017, we ran an all day civic imagination symposium in Bowling Green, Kentucky. The event brought together community members concerned about the changing nature of work in the state. Though our participants certainly had a shared concern, they didn't necessarily agree on how to tackle the challenges they faced. To engage the perspectives in the room, we had to be sensitive in handling divisive terms and dystopian stories as they surfaced. We also had to listen for silences as much as we listened to what was said. And, we had to acknowledge the role that fear, specifically fear of the future, played in stifling creativity. This was a sensitive session with high stakes that taught us a lot about the civic imagination and dissent.

## Introduction

When Tom[1] participated in our workshop session in Bowling Green, Kentucky, he talked about his working class family history, his roots in Appalachia, and his

---

1. Names participants have been anonymized to protect their identities.

uncertainty about a future he saw for himself and others in the region. At one point, he even pulled out a 1977 Time Magazine and pointed to the man, a miner, featured on the cover. This was his uncle, he shared. To Tom, his uncle reminded him of the changes that had forced many "to finally explore a world where coal jobs—and jobs in general—are scarce." Reluctantly, he too would accept moving forward if the region's "proud past, deeply rooted in faith, family and work ethic" would be honored." In other words, to know where he was going, Tom needed to remember where he came from.

Tom participated in day-long workshop on the future of work in Kentucky that we ran in September 2017. Like others, he had experienced the decline of the coal and tobacco industries personally. For decades, these industries had provided secure, well paid jobs that lasted a lifetime and beyond. Their decline (from 48,000 to 18,000 jobs over 30 years for coal mining) and a sense that future jobs will require new skills and relocation greatly destabilized local communities. Available employment statistics from Kentucky confirm the bleak economic outlook: 17.2% of Kentucky's population lives in poverty, and 34.5% of working class families live under 200% of the poverty line (Spotlight on Poverty 2019). On top of this, images depicting impoverishment and narratives of lives broken by unemployment and opioid addictions dominate mainstream media, fueling fear, and even despair, when it comes to thinking of what the future may hold for Kentucky.

## Future of Work Initiative

We brought the participants together to support the launch of a networked Future of Work Initiative, an effort initiated by Kentucky native, MIT graduate, and former VP of Innovation at the media company Fusion, Sam Ford. Building on his deep understanding of participatory practices, Ford took a distinctly interdisciplinary approach to the future of work in Kentucky, that responded to his observation that it is hard to get excited about the future, when it does not seem to include you. The session we co-hosted with Ford sought to initiate the process of building a more inclusive and participatory vision of the future that would include, rather than exclude Kentuckians. As Ford noted during an interview with the Boston Globe:

> Coal miners and laid-off line workers don't need 'job reskilling,' they need to learn to think differently. They need to realize that they possess unique aptitudes that can be applied to 21st-century jobs. (Ford cited in Howe 2017)

In that same interview, Rusty Justice, former miner and founder of BitSource, a coding company, made a similar observation when he noted that, the miners he retrains to be coders do not only need to pick up new skills, they also need to understand that "coal is not the soul of who they are." For Justice, "re-imagination" is ultimately just as important as learning new skills.

Like Justice and Ford, everyone in the room that day cared about the changing nature of work in Kentucky. Some of our participants worried about the disappearance of jobs like mining and tobacco farming and the social, human, and economic upheaval these changes brought. We also had educators who were concerned about training young people for jobs in this rapidly changing environment. Others were busy brainstorming and engaging with innovative entrepreneurship models that would bring new forms of employment to the region. They all knew people who had already lost their jobs. Some participants had already met each other; most had not.

## Reconciling Future Visions

Given these realities, we intentionally walked into this workshop with an open mind. We knew that we wanted to deepen our approach to the civic imagination by strengthening *connections* between the past, present, and future. We were also aware that our workshop framework grew out of our work with mostly young (or at least younger) communities. With significant caveats around issues like LGBTQ (which were particularly contentious in the American Muslim context) or reproductive rights (like the abortion issues that divided some of the youth affiliated with Invisible Children), our previous collaborations also skewed towards progressive groups. Our participants in Bowling Green represented a different participant community. They were a stark mix of Democrats and Republicans, and included Trump supporters. They were also primarily white and skewed older. In fact, our oldest participant was well into his seventies, a fact that he wore like a badge of honor.

The day was divided into four parts. We began by going around the room and inviting all the participants to introduce themselves by sharing a work-related memory object that evoked something about their past in relation to labor and work. Henry Jenkins then shared some background about the Civic Imagination Project. We followed this with the Infinite Hope workshop and concluded the day with a debrief focused on possible next steps for the fledgling initiative.

The future world imagined through the brainstorm bore some similarities to the technologically driven visions of future worlds our other workshops had yielded. A portion of the room was committed to finding solutions to transportation barriers, particularly those faced by the elderly. Driverless cars, shared ownership of vehicles and exoskeletal walking to allow people to promote longevity all demonstrated a desire for convenience. Fried chicken would be healthy. Food would be tasty and nutritious and could be delivered through an Uber-like platform. We would all have excellent teeth and would be able to 3-D print organ replacements on demand. Education would be adaptable to students' needs, and we would all have a better work-life balance where we could 'unplug' from being connected.

At the same time, some participants resisted such futuristic departures. For example, one participant wanted to continue to drive his own car, just drive it faster and without dealing with traffic. Others foresaw that businesses would become a key funder of higher education in the future, predictably focusing more explicitly on applicable skill development. Education would also operate through a fully integrated apprenticeship model. This would be a future where we would telecommute and be universally connected through an advanced form of broadband.

The productive tensions surfaced through this brainstorm helped manifest the various world-views and life experiences present in the room. They also helped us see how ideas that seemed completely different could connect in surprising ways. A debate that emerged around the future of welfare is a case in point. One participant proposed that all welfare should be ended by 2040. This prompted another participant to object and argue that many individuals and families need it. This was followed by a brief, somewhat tense, exchange, which resulted in an agreement that in the ideal future welfare would be abolished BECAUSE it would no be longer needed.

Reconciling such tensions, surfacing surprising consensus, and ultimately starting to chart a tentative way forward set the tone for the day.

## Past as Lens for the Future

Our participants were very emotionally connected to the memory objects they brought to introduce themselves to the group. They shared family stories and histories that clearly mattered a lot to them, that they cared about deeply. They also made some surprising connections with each other as they introduced themselves. For example, one participant's first employer in a sheet metal fabrication workshop turned out to be another participant's grandfather!

Overwhelmingly, the memory objects revealed how intricately memories of work were tied to the local participants' sense of family, community and place. Matt, co-founder of a rural online news site, brought in a Peabody "trinket" as it reminded him of this father, who, in Matt's words, "worked third shift seven days a week for Peabody for 23 years." He went on to share his memories of Christmases where he tried to sleep in as long as possible to make sure he would wake up to see his father return from his night shift. Jane, another participant, shared a photo of her high school graduation because she was the first person in her family to get a diploma. She shared this as the introduced herself:

> My daddy can't read and can barely even sign his own name, but he can tell you how to make a tarp, how to service a semi, and how to train horses. My father-in-law is also illiterate, but he is one of the best mechanics around. My father-in-law is a third-generation heavy equipment mechanic—my husband is the fourth. They were all taught trades by their fathers at a young age, and through experience and hard work, have had successful careers. In my parents' generation, and certainly their parents before them, an education was not necessary to have a good job or be good at what you do.

Reflecting on changes she has witnessed growing up she continued:

> These days, a college education is often required even for blue-collar jobs. Don't get me wrong, having an education is very important, but it's not for everyone. Not everyone has "book smarts", but maybe they can look at a diesel engine and instantly understand how it works. When this picture was taken, kids that took machine shop, electrical, automotive and carpentry were often surrounded by a stigma that they weren't smart or weren't good at school. A lot of them weren't great at school work, but they were and are great at their trades. Those trades are the backbone of our society, so it's important to continue to promote and offer these skills to our children.

Even as Jane celebrated her own academic achievement, she remained committed to recognizing the skills that defined the generation of her parents, and just importantly, the respect that they commanded. She made clear that her own break with that tradition has not changed her respect for those trades.

Though very different, Marcie's description of her Smith-Corona Super 12 typewriter, brought up similar issues. She recalled:

> I stumbled upon this typewriter in a thrift store, sitting next to an abandoned mismatched living room set. It doesn't work perfectly—it's badly in need of service repairs—but I didn't care as I lovingly cleaned each key the second I got it home.

Though she never actually used it, Marcie looked at the typewriter as a reminder that "it's important to get back to our roots, to polish up what was working well and borrow from that past, let it inspire us, to bring ourselves toward a brighter future." Strikingly, Marcie admitted that her typewriter has "no real functioning purpose anymore". It just reminded her of "where we've been and to… keep moving forward." For both Marcie and Jane, connections of the past mattered. Though things have clearly changed, their personal narratives are tinged with a desire to restore, or at least retain, elements of their past.

A similar relationship between the present and the past emerged in the "Love Real Music" story created by one of the groups during the story making portion of the workshop. Set in 2040, the story centered on Northwest, a daughter of Kim Kardashian and Kanye West, who feels her life has been a waste. She decides to pursue a musical career and consults with an aging Lady Gaga who encourages her to create music that connects the future to the past by using real instruments from the past, which had been thought to be useless and outdated. Northwest begins learning to play the piano and is eventually able to make a living by becoming a musician. To launch her career she decides to use a rubber mallet as a symbol from the past that can inform skills of the future.

## Commitment to the Present

For some workshop participants imagining the world of 2040 was hard as they felt they did not want to move past the present and all it represented in their lives. They wanted to hold on to things and people that mattered to them, and they found it difficult to sort through what to keep and what to leave behind. As we already mentioned, driving his truck was very important to one of our participants. It was something he loved to do. Because of this, he hesitated to embrace any innovation (like driverless cars) that could potentially infringe on his ability to engage in what he so enjoyed. Another participant felt a similar connection to the meat dishes she loved and did not want to have to give them up in the future to accommodate another participant's proposed "plant based" cuisine.

In both cases, we urged these participants to drill deeper to articulate more specifically what they liked in the present to help us start to develop futures that could accommodate the ideas proposed by other participants. We asked the participant who loved his truck if he could envision an improvement to this experience? "I want to drive my truck faster," he responded. So, what if his truck were a zero emissions vehicle? What if it also was much easier to operate? And, of course, it would also go faster. Would that be ok? "Yes," he conceded. We asked the participant concerned about holding on to food she loved, what if you didn't need to compromise between taste and nutrition? Your favorite food could taste the same. It would just be healthy too. Would that work for you? She nodded her head, but did not appear to be fully convinced yet.

We continued to support participants as they thought through how what was important to them today could be reconciled with the future visions they had collectively generated. Eventually, they started to see how the things they valued today (and even those from the past) did not need to block them from imagining aspirational futures. For example, one group's story introduced New Way

University, a learning institution that bridged between the present and the future. Through several enacted scenes, the group shared the story of a young woman who had lost her job and returned to university to acquire skills that enabled her to find new employment. She was able to received skills-based training through flexible programs that were offered at the university and eventually found a new and better job. Though this story, the groups sketched out a tentative future where older structures could support the emergence of new formats in higher education.

## Words Divide

All day, language triggered disagreements as politicized terms like "welfare" and "healthcare" forced participants to fall back into predetermined partisan positions. Getting them to emerge again was challenging, as some phrases proved to be particularly divisive. These included "single payer health system", "falling through the cracks", and "socialism". Still, moving the conversation further out into the future forced our participants to find new words to describe what they cared about, a process that resulted in surprising agreement on key issues. This was most striking when we asked what health could look like in 2040. The elimination of disease and increased longevity were at the top of the list for everyone. The participants also wanted more transparent cost structures. They wanted to understand cost upfront. Some participants wanted care to be free; everyone wanted to be able to afford it. Everyone also wanted to have access to care that was outcome, rather than service based.

Though they agreed on the general parameters of what a desirable future for health, and healthcare, could look like, the participants hit an impasse when it came to thinking through possible scenarios that would move us in that direction. They struggled to find words to describe a model of change as terms like single payer, affordable, universal were irreversibly tainted as partisan.

## Fear in the Room

Fear stifles the imagination. And, fear was certainly present during our workshop in Bowling Green. We saw it when the participants shared their memory objects and connected them to soon-to-be-extinct professions that had defined their families for generations. Fear was very much a part of the pain and loss that accompanied many of these stories, and grim predictions around the automation of labor and disappearing jobs were present in the room all day. At moments, the fear-inducing specter of unemployment took over the room, crippling all imagination. At one point, a participant even stood up and recited a list of jobs that would likely cease to exist in the next decade. Farmers. Bank tellers. Postal Service Carriers. Fast food cooks. Typists. Assembly line workers. File clerks. Cashiers. The list went on.

Distrust and trepidation came through in the stories the groups created, and technology often played an ambivalent, and inevitable, role. In Joe Schmo Gets a Job, technology was, literally, invasive. This was a story of Joe, who lost the job he had for twenty years. He applies for job with Uber, as he needs to make money somehow. Before he can begin to work for them, he is told to get a health checkup, where he learns that he needs to get an implant put inside him to monitor his health (and him) at all times. This monitor will send the information directly to his employer as well. The implant is not supposed to have any side effects. "What could go wrong?" the health worker asks as she installs it. But, the implant does cause Joe significant discomfort, particularly as it is a miniature-bull that now sits right under his skin. A hacker is also able to hack into Joe's data and gain control over his body. Joe loses his job again. At this point, technology has quite literally destroyed his health and robbed him of his wealth. Luckily, Joe is able to connect with a lawyer who takes on his case. She files a lawsuit and gets the implants abolished. Joe is able to get his job back, and patients across the country gain more privacy rights when it comed to their medical information. This was a grim and technologically dystopian future for the average worker.

## Where Can We Go from Here?

Though our workshop in Bowling Green yielded useful insights about the participants' shared aspirations, it also revealed a break down when it came to identifying mechanisms of change, or how change could be accomplished. Some participants cautiously put their faith in lone actors or super heroes (think Iron Man) to save the day. Others tentatively looked to compromised solutions offered by large corporations like an Amazon or Google. No one identified public institutions, politicians, or civil associations as solution providers. Overall, the participants' stories were extremely skeptical of our ability to move forward. Some even retreated into Stephen Duncombe's "tyranny of the possible" when it came of imagining how change happens. For many of them, there simply was no way out.

In the final session of the day, the participants brought the ideas generated during the day to the questions, opportunities and challenges they face in Kentucky. They seemed almost relieved to be able to focus on more immediate issues. They talked about how the current course offerings at the university do not meet re-training needs of returning students. They also talked about needing to help people re-define who they are, to help them understand that they do not need to only be defined by their occupation.

Finally, the conversation turned to Kentucky, as a divided state that needs to work towards a more united approach to the future of work. "Kentucky is a dining table with all the chairs facing out" was a metaphor our participants used to describe the state's three distinct cultural regions (the Midwest, the South, and Appalachia) and a border shared with seven other states. They also wanted to connect western and eastern Kentucky with the more prosperous center of the state (called the "Golden Triangle" locally).

As the day drew to a close, they conceded that the inhabitants of Kentucky needed to write a new narrative for themselves, to help them move towards a future vision they all saw as desirable. "When you give them a job, you give them a hope" one participant quipped. They agreed they all needed hope, especially when the world around them filled them with fear.

# Bibliography

Duncombe, Stephen. 2012. "Utopia is No Place" Open Field: Conversations on the Common (in conversation with Sarah Peters). August 27. https://walkerart.org/magazine/stephen-duncombe-utopia-open-field

Howe, Jeff. 2017. "Kentucky Wants MIT to Stop Destroying Its Jobs. MIT Is Listening" Boston Globe, November 15. https://www.bostonglobe.com/magazine/2017/11/14/hard-excited-about-future-work-you-don-think-you/6qgQL8Rlbq0waMXyhrTxkK/story.html

Spotlight on Poverty and Opportunity. 2019. "Kentucky State Government" spotlightonpoverty.org/states/Kentucky (accessed on October 30, 2019)

# CHAPTER SEVEN

# Future of Faith?— Fayetteville, Arkansas

## KEY INSIGHTS

Our workshop at the Good Shepherd Lutheran Church in Fayetteville, Arkansas explored how imagination intersects with faith and spirituality. In this particular session, consensus around progressive Christian values led to a clearer articulation of aspirational future worlds rooted in a commitment to social justice. Building on this, the participants strategized how the insights gained could move them forward in cultivating more sustained productive collaborations with other aligned communities, leading to an effort that eventually contributed to the forming of the New Sactuary Coalition of Northwest Arkansas.

## Introduction

> *"The story begins in the not so distant future. An orange haired demon has taken over the world. He is in charge of everything and has made the world an evil place. In a mutiny, he is overcome by angels of virtue who surround him and implant a heart shaped rock, changing his world view. He shifts towards being more accountable, more generous."*

An "orange haired demon" and "angels of virtue" were the central characters in one of the performances created by participants in a future world workshop we ran at the Good Shepherd Lutheran Church in Fayetteville, Arkansas on October 27, 2017. As the performance reached its climax and the demon was transformed into a kinder being, other workshop participants applauded enthusiastically to express their approval for this barely masked political critique and Christian-themed happy ending.

For us, the Fayetteville workshop offered an opportunity to work with a religious Christian community for the first time, and we were keen to learn about the how civic imagination would resonate in this context. More generally, we wanted to understand how faith connects with the imagination, particularly in relation to civic issues. For Clint Schnekloth, the Church's pastor, the workshop offered a chance to strengthen his congregation's commitment to social issues. He also wanted to explore how he might be able to use the civic imagination to build alliances with other civically oriented communities in the area. About half of the 30 workshop participants were members of Schenkloth's congregation. To that end, our workshop at the Good Shepherd included memory objects, a future world-building workshop, and a post workshop debrief.

## Faith and Social Justice

When he assumed leadership of the Good Shepherd, Schnekloth made his commitment to social justice known to his congregation. He regularly preached on civic topics and collaborated with local non-profits around issues like marriage equality and immigration reform. Schnekloth's commitment to social issues connects to his identity as a Christian. He articulates his commitment to social justice as a key tenet of his Christianity on his blog:

> When Christians in our tradition make vows at their baptism, the last thing they promise is to work for justice and peace in all the world. It is this final vow of baptism that is especially squashed by our culture ....If justice is what love looks like in public, then in addition to the private familial love we are called to practice in our families and places of worship, we are called at the civic level and in the polis to works of justice, which is the form of love in public life." (Clint Schnekloth—http://lutheranconfessions.blogspot.com/2018/05/)

Given Schnekloth's focus on social issues, we were not surprised when our civic imagination session led to a strikingly coherent expression of shared values among the participants. We were also delighted to see how surfacing such a consensus around progressive Christian values could lead to a clearer articulation of aspirational future worlds that could then in turn support deeper collaboration with aligned communities.

## A Future World Defined by Social Justice

Social issues and ensuring equity and equality soon emerged as a central theme for the world of 2060 created by our participants. Key characteristics of this world included a basic income for all people with disabilities, universal access to food, end of mass incarceration, guaranteed housing for everyone, respect for education, and healed racial divisions. This was a world in which all people were valued as humans, where diversity was celebrated and compassion and empathy (rather than partisan affiliations) drove relationships. Fear no longer dictated our decisions. Eventually, this shift in interpersonal relationships led to a peaceful world, with greatly diminished policing budgets as no, or very little, law enforcement would be needed.

Establishing social justice as a central organizing value of their future allowed the participants to create an internally coherent world. This was a world where access to health care would become a basic human right. This care would be affordable and more preventive than reactive. All healthcare related systems would be reoriented to focus on care rather than profit. All humans would be able to travel, and even immigrate to new places. In fact, travel would be an integral part of all education to allow people to experience other cultures as a requisite training for the values that govern this new world.

In a similar vein, this would be a future world where people would get to work in meaningful occupations, uncoupled from huge income disparities. But more importantly, individuals would not be defined by their work; their life would have a deeper intellectual and spiritual meaning.

Some of the participants even advocated for a future world in which social consciousness would also be applied to all living things and our planet to reverse climate change and refreeze the north and south poles. They expressed a deep desire for a world in balance, where agriculture does not harm the environment and where buildings are living things.

## Imagining a Future for Faith

As our future world brainstorm drew to a close, we noticed that no one had explicitly brought up the future of faith and religion as a separate category. So, we asked the participants directly, "What does faith look like in 2060?" The question seemed to catch our workshop participants somewhat off guard. A silence fell over the room.

"A planned obsolescence of religious institutions," one participant finally offered, after a brief hesitation. Others considered this proposal and postulated that, perhaps, we will be able to achieve a deeper, socially conscious spirituality, which will make institutions unnecessary. Soon, as the group warmed up to this idea, they imagined that networks and faith-based communities could be very important in their envisioned future. Connecting various faith-based communities would, in fact, enable shared humanity to emerge, leading to the creation of an entity that could eventually exceed our understanding of how faith and religion operate today. In this vision, faith, abstracted from the religious institutions of the current moment, would serve as the underlying value system that informs shared agendas and goals around the world. Churches (and other religious institutions) could still exist in such a world, but would become mediators of social justice.

Notably, the participants agreed that faith would still be needed in this future world, as people will still want to find meaning for their lives. Networked faith communities, rather than formal religious institutions, would support people in their personal spiritual journeys. Diverse faith traditions would return to their underlying core values. Christians would reaffirm their key religious principles like caring for the poor, loving your neighbor, and respecting children. Crucially, faith, as such, would not prescribe the imagination; rather it would serve as a starting place for its expression, within a realization that "something bigger is going on" in the world.

This commitment to finding shared values beyond the current limits of religion and discovering new shared languages of faith came to life in the stories the participants created. "I have faith like a milkweed seed, flying around," one group chanted as they entered the stage. This was a story about a future moment when farmers destroy the milkweed and threaten the existence of the monarch butterfly. Drawn together by a need to take corrective action, a group of students and academics collaborated to solve the problem. They apply their knowledge of science to resolve the issue and are able to restore the milkweed and heal the butterfly. It then rises again to become a symbol of their sensitive, sustainable, spiritual and compassionate community.

## Ties to the Past

Though they eagerly envisioned a future world based on their shared values, our Fayetteville participants also felt it was important to hold on to their past. Many of them were committed to remembering their families and loved ones, and treasured the memories they had shared.

The importance of memories came through in the stories they created. In one such story, a grandmother tells her granddaughters stories of the Marshall Islands (the grandmother was played by a female participant from the Marshall Islands). She tells her stories of the past where there was clean water and people did not need to worry. Esther (the grand daughter) is so moved by the idea of clean water being available, that she tells her friends at school about how marvelous and wonderful that time long ago was. All the friends start to think about how to make clean water readily available again. They decide to start a clean water movement and come up with a slogan: "clean water for you, clean water for me". Her determination to reach into the past to build a better future results in the development of affordable water filters that everyone can use.

Similarly, remembering and honoring family ties was a common theme in the memory objects the participants used to introduce themselves to the group. Noah, a female participant in her early 60s, described a quilt that her grandmother had made. She shared how its texture connected her to "her spirit" and through it to her family history. For another older female participant, a paperweight that she had made for her own father when she was a child in the 1960s took on a similar meaning. She explained that her father had kept the paperweight with him until he died, at which point she discovered it when she was going through his things. She explained how having the paperweight in her possession now brings her "great joy". For these two, and other, participants, the memory objects they shared served as entry points into their past that also strongly informed their current and future world aspirations.

## Towards Faith-Based Civic Imagination

As the participants reflected on their workshop experience, they appreciated how entering through the imagination had helped free them from their usual constraints. They cherished the opportunity to work together and noted that everyone had felt invited to contribute to the creative process. They told us that we made them feel hopeful at a time where they often felt despair over the current state of affairs.

At the end of the day, the group spent time discussing how the workshop had helped them surface shared values that could support their continued participation in a growing progressive Christian movement. To Schnekloth, the workshop provided a starting place for the group as they moved forward in articulating what such a movement could look like and how the imagination could support sustained engagement.

Some participants urged us to think about expanding the participant pool to include other, even more conservative Christian communities. One participant was struck by how powerful it would be if she could bring more conservative members of her family to this workshop. She shared that members of her family did not talk about politics when they met, which made it impossible for them to find common ground. "So, maybe civic imagination workshops could help them identify shared values?" she asked. The participants stressed that civic imagination (and our workshop) could help them continue to build empathy with other communities to help build a more sustained connection between otherwise disparate civic communities and efforts.

As we concluded the session that day, we realized that the insights generated by the participants had pushed our thinking about the civic imagination. For one, the session had forced us to acknowledge that the invitation to imagine possibilities and surface inspiring stories would likely tap participants' faith-based beliefs. We needed to be more aware of this in our sessions. We also realized that acknowledging religion and belief as sources of inspiration openly in our workshops would help participants feel more comfortable with sharing faith-based narratives during the sessions. Finally, we were left with a curiosity about the connections between faith and the imagination, which we plan to explore more fully one day. In the meantime, we have made it a point to take note of where, how and why faith and religion surfaces in our discussions.

## Building a Network through a Civic Imagination Event

A year later, we asked Clint Schnekloth to reflect on the session we ran at the Good Shepherd Lutheran Church. He noted that having us come and facilitate the session in person as outsiders "was especially helpful" because "we were personally connecting with you guys and hosting you." Schnekloth felt our physical presence had the "net effect of increasing participation and interest."

Schnekloth also recalled how that there had been "a lot of reporting back from the participants about how therapeutic it was for them to participate" in the event. Our workshop took place at a time when President Trump's more punitive policies (termination of DACA and TPS and the Muslim travel ban) started to go into effect, which he saw as "particularly stressful to a lot of the people" who came to the workshop because many of them were personally impacted by the administration's actions or knew people who were. To him, being part of the workshop itself was the most valuable part of the experience for participants. The workshop became an event that brought people together and invited them to collectively imagine aspirational futures at a moment when the world around them deflated their morale. To him, the event fulfilled its function when the participants emerged more connected, motivated and refreshed.

Schnekloth went on to run a few other civic imagination workshops with faith leaders and community leaders in the year that followed as a part of his effort to collaboratively create the New Sanctuary Coalition in Northwest Arkansas and noted that the sessions he organized there had a similar effect on participants. He explained that:

> It's not uncommon for faith leaders to get together for meetings. But we tend to jump into the business right away, of whatever it is we're gathering for. And so, it was a very fast and effective way to step back to more of who are we in the room with? What are they like? What do they bring? That kind of thing.

Our workshop was stronger because it did not immediately "result in the group as a whole chasing down the next step". Schnekloth's reflection clarified how an approach rooted in the civic imagination could fit within the larger arc of campaign and network building. Our workshops could become the creative event that jump-starts collaboration between individuals, communities, and organizations. Civic imagination could then help movements coalesce, connect, and gain momentum. Beyond this, other supports are clearly needed to sustain momentum over time. Our experiences in Fayetteville and sustained dialogue with Schnekloth expanded our thinking as we continued to develop our approaches. Knowing about what worked well and where our approach faltered was extremely helpful as we defined what we hope to accomplish through the civic imagination.

## Bibliography

Schnekloth, Clint. 2018. "How to Do All the Christian Things". *Lutheran Confessions Blog*. http://lutheranconfessions.blogspot.com/2018/05/ (accessed on June 19, 2019).

# CHAPTER EIGHT

# Pakistan, from the Heart: Civic Imagination in Context of Violent Extremism

## KEY INSIGHTS

Our partnership with HIVE, a community focused non-profit[1], allowed us to apply civic imagination to "Counter Violent Extremism" efforts in Pakistan. Between 2016 and 2017, HIVE worked with us to explore how Pakistanis imagine futures as they conducted interviews, ran Infinite Hope workshops, and launched aspirational grassroots community projects across the country.

## Introduction

*"Pakistan's culture is so rich, deep and diverse that even in 2060, Pakistan has not forgotten its culture. Pakistan has not progressed like the Western countries. Pakistan has not been inspired by the Western lifestyle or Western culture that you're talking about because its deep rooted culture has always been affected by people still respecting their families, people are still caring for each other. Due to this mighty power of caring for each other, we've developed at very rapid scale. Today's community of 2060 is better compared to the past because we are not concerned about judging others or judging other people's beliefs or religious inclination. Violence has been ruled out." (Dil Say Pakistan interview respondent)*

1. This account was written with research insight from Syed Ali Abbas Zaidi and Maha Usman.

This aspirational vision of Pakistan in 2060 emerged through interviews conducted by HIVE, an organization dedicated to "training, research, resource development, and social innovation to counter extremism and work towards an inclusive, peaceful society." HIVE's interviews were part of Dil Say Pakistan (Pakistan, from the Heart), a national campaign that sought to shift perceptions of Pakistan and Pakistanis within the country. Along with the interviews, HIVE ran 28 civic imagination workshops with 1181 youth participants who were between the ages of 18–25. These workshops also led to the funding of 57 social action projects proposed by participants who were directly inspired to act because of this experience.

In 2016 and 2017, our team collaborated with HIVE on the creation, administration, and analysis of these interviews and workshops. This was a joint effort that moved their project forward while providing us with valuable learnings about the civic imagination along the way. For us, this collaboration also modeled how the civic imagination might be applied to support sector specific initiatives in other locations.

We first met members of the Dil Say Pakistan (DSP) team through Media Meets Message, a transmedia for social change training experience we helped organize at the University of Southern California in January, 2016. The three-week program was comprised of five teams of creative media professionals from around the world. We designed the curriculum to explore various media-based approaches to social change and invited participants to consider how some of these practices could apply to their own projects. We also introduced all of the participants to the civic imagination through our worldbuilding workshops and other related presentations and activities.

Our approach really clicked with the team from Pakistan and led to a sustained collaboration that extended beyond Media Meets Message. The Dil Say Pakistan team was comprised of well-known documentary filmmakers, producers, community activists, grassroots film festival organizers, and a popular music celebrity. Several members of the team had already collaborated to create the animated television series *Burka Avenger*, a program about a teacher at a girls' school who becomes a superhero by night, wearing the burka to mask her identity. The show is all about creating a positive cultural vision of education for women and girls in Pakistan and is a powerful example of civic imagination in its own right.

The makers of the Dil Say Pakistan campaign lamented that Pakistanis had allowed themselves to be defined by problems of poverty, violence and intolerance and that these tendencies were perpetuated through journalism and media. They believed in telling uplifting stories that reflected positive sides of Pakistan; its people, history, and culture.

Drawing on these insights and the team's areas of expertise, content created through Dil Say Pakistan included a signature music video, travelogues featuring the accomplishments of ordinary people, 60 second films celebrating everyday heroes, an animated series in which the world is saved from destruction through evidence of people's good deeds, and community based street theater.

## Pakistan and CVE

The dominant negative narratives and frameworks that the Dil Say Pakistan campaign was working against in their project need to be understood through the lens of "CVE" which is the wonkish shorthand for "Countering Violent Extremism." In 2015, CVE was generally defined as a "broad-ranging term that describes initiatives to reduce the spread of violent extremist ideologies" and was positioned as a multifaceted response to "radicalization" efforts that "may result from a multitude of "push" and "pull" factors such as poverty, ethnic or sectarian discord, political grievances, and extremist ideologies" (Mirahmadi et al. 2016, 190). As Mirahmadi and his co-authors further observe:

> Radical ideologies continue to gain traction in Pakistan, and the risk to civilians, government institutions, and aid organizations is growing in spite of the Pakistani military's counter-extremism and de-radicalization programs.

As area expert Saira Mano Orakzai (2017, 1–2) notes, Pakistan "became a focal point of terrorism after 9/11" and counter measures have generally "focused on military measures along with pouring billions of dollars into development and peacebuilding measures supported by the international community."

The Dil Say Pakistan campaign, funded through international donor grants, recognized that CVE initiatives needed to be more representative and aligned with people's real aspirations to be truly effective. Although the problems of violence were vividly real, the very term "CVE" already cedes some power to the ideologies it seeks to dislodge by establishing its efforts as "counter and against" rather than being generative of a new and different set of values and approaches. This was why the Dil Say Pakistan team was so inspired by the civic imagination framework. They saw that it could provide them with an alternative approach to address the real problems in their country.

For Syed Ali Abbas Zaidi, HIVE's founder and the person responsible for the community facing aspects of the Dil Say Pakistan campaign, the civic imagination framework presented a bottom-to-top emancipatory model that could ultimately support more community ownership of CVE interventions. As Zaidi pointed out during one of our conversations, religious extremists have long used future-oriented strategies to inspire people to subscribe to visions of society aligned with their value systems. Supporting this claim more broadly, research by Charlie

Winter (2015, 28) established that ISIS's online propaganda pushed state-building and civic life in a highly sophisticated fashion as a part of their "apocalyptic utopianism." Zaidi's goals of building positive counter-narratives from the ground up in the context of Pakistan (where the Taliban, not ISIS, is the dominant threat) is aligned with other experts working in this space. For example, Basit (2015), and Mahmadi et al. (2016) talk about the need for community-based and inclusive approaches to CVE that acknowledge there are unrecognized majorities of citizens that do not buy into the messages and ideals of terrorist organizations; that the values and perspectives of such groups and communities should be tapped and made visible as an organic countervailing force to the threats of violent extremism.

Working with us, HIVE used civic imagination to better understand what elements of their current situation Pakistanis want to change, what they value, what narratives motivate them, and what they see as a desirable outcome of change when they think of their futures. HIVE hoped that what they learned would eventually inform the creation of "a movement activating people against violent extremism". To that end, and with our support, HIVE fielded a multi-part qualitative study that sought to surface key narrative tropes present among urban Pakistani youth (as they were a key target group for the campaign). They also ran civic imagination workshops all over the country throughout the campaign and used these to invite participants to imagine a positive future for Pakistan. Workshop participants were also invited to submit small scale project proposals inspired by their worldbuilding experience. Proposals selected by HIVE received seed funding.

## What We Learned from the Interviews

Our civic imagination themed interviews were conducted in Pakistan by HIVE members with urban youth and civically active youth leaders. They were carried out early on in the Dil Say Pakistan campaign so that the findings could inform subsequent media creation and community building efforts. The interviews taught us a lot about how engaging with the questions, paradoxes and challenges that arise from aspirational thinking can inform grassroots social change initiatives. Here are the key insights surfaced through this collaboration:

Meaning of Pakistan—Many of the young people had a love-hate relationship with their homeland. As one respondent noted, "Pakistan is obviously home, there is nothing better than Pakistan. But, I think Pakistan is a shit-hole as well." At the same time, some respondents mentioned positive things they associate with Pakistan such as supportive family systems, traditional food, music, and freedom. In the words of one respondent, Pakistan means "liking cricket, it means liking chai, it means joking with one friend in Punjabi and one friend in Pushto ....It's the everyday experiences that make Pakistan." Other respondents talked about corruption, extremism, terrorism and a regressive economy. This sentiment was summarized by one of the respondents in the following exchange during an interview:

> Interviewer: "What does Pakistan mean to you?
> *Respondent: Hell*
> Interviewer: Why?
> *Respondent: Because every day I encounter such stories, I face such experiences, I hardly get any good news from someone, even from my neighbors, or TV and social media." (Phase 1 interview respondent)*

When asked about the perception of Pakistan outside of the country, nearly all respondents talked about how Pakistan is viewed as a backward terrorist haven. In fact, most of the respondents cited negative perceptions of Pakistan internationally as a key and demoralizing concern.

**Visions of Pakistan 2060**—We asked the respondents to engage in an exercise where they imagined an aspirational future for Pakistan. Though this exercise proved to be quite challenging, as these examples reveal, the visions surfaced commitment to a future where Pakistan's particular interpretation of democracy has been allowed to thrive:

> "The politicians have realized that they need to put the country's interests first. They have let democracy flow. They have taken a strong stance on things where they would otherwise cave in. Institutions have grown stronger, like education. The judiciary system would be competent, just, fair and doing their work on time. That is the biggest problem in Pakistan. It won't be a case of justice-delayed, justice-denied. I would go for reform rather than a revolution.

> "The Pakistan of 2060 is an ideal Pakistan for me. In terms of governance I would like to see a fluid democracy. This also means abolishing the feudal system, which is literally ruling over people through bonded labor. I do realize a 100% pure democracy is not possible. I would like to see it flowing. I always tell to my friends that Zardari's government is the only one that lasted 5 years in the 65 year history of Pakistan. I still think we are in the evolution phase. We look at countries like England and the West and want a democracy like that, but they evolved over a period of 600 to 700 years. I see a lot democratic evolution happening."

Read together, the visions for 2060 surfaced many shared aspirations, including a desire for transparent media, a free and improved education system, increased social mobility, no corruption, and strong cultural identity. As the above cited excerpts suggest, respondents also wanted a fluid (uniquely constructed) democracy in Pakistan. Overall, the respondents were hopeful about the future of Pakistan but saw progress as contingent upon structural and societal changes that need to take place urgently. To the Dil Say Pakistan team, this 'hope' of a better future presented a real opportunity for tapping the imaginations of Pakistani youth. As such, the project demonstrated how a vision of a better tomorrow, a holistic solution that encompasses civic life, political matters, cultural evolution and social issues, could be embedded within CVE messages.

**Models of Change**—Though the respondents cited a broad range of possibilities for how change might happen in the country, the models of change surfaced through the interviews overwhelmingly highlighted a collective movement rooted in existing community ties. As one respondent said, Pakistan would achieve its aspirational future "by getting your voice and story to as many people as possible and creating a pool of positive and empowered people that break the hold of the negative thought leaders." In his words, this would be a "bottom to top effort," and new leaders would emerge from outside the current political spheres. Similarly, other respondents felt that the (educated) youth would mobilize for change as "nobody can bring the change except us." Strikingly, the respondents did not identify particular leaders in this process, rather they imagined that the "thousands of people [will] have sacrificed their lives to make us reach this day." Breaking down this grassroots change model, the participants pointed to specific efforts that are already working towards this aspirational future, they include: a collective effort for women empowerment, better community engagement, effective social media messaging, and awareness campaigns. Technological solutions to existing problems were notably absent from the responses.

Based on these insights, the HIVE team concluded that patriotic sentiments presented important opportunities for a CVE campaign to tap alternative, future oriented, and progressive approaches to supporting young Pakistani's collective. Existing nation building efforts are often focused on exclusivity (who cannot be Pakistani) and confrontation (fueled by anti-Indian nationalistic rhetoric), which is largely reactive and relies on pre-existing frames.

## Story-Making Workshops Build a Foundation

Through 28 workshops, participants were asked to create stories set in the future that manifested their aspirations. A review of the stories collected revealed a real need for confidence and collective identity building around what it means to be Pakistani, further supporting the findings of the initial interviews.

As participants envisioned a Pakistan that would be "free from threats," that would "win World Cups" in sports, and where Pakistani entrepreneurs would invent the "flying car," they demonstrated the power of the civic imagination as a tool to support individual and collective empowerment. The models of change undergirding such progress were based on religious harmony, enjoyable education for all, Pakistani writers inspiring the whole world, and the abilities of all people to contribute to the positive development of the nation.

In the post workshop survey, HIVE also asked people to surface two examples of inspiring stories that they had witnessed in their local communities. Many of the stories submitted mentioned social action as a key to the path towards a brighter and more peaceful future for Pakistan. Most of the issues mentioned in the stories were related to poverty, economic inequalities, and health issues (including first aid efforts in emergency contexts). Participants were also inspired by accounts of social action geared towards community development including welfare, access to clean drinking water, clean environment, and education. Although faith did not surface directly in these accounts, it is interesting to note that there was a great resonance with people performing positive social actions because of religious narratives that reward people (sawaab).

## From Workshops to Projects

All HIVE workshop participants were invited to submit mini-project "Social Challenge" proposals to start to 'activate' the vision of Pakistan surfaced during sessions. Over 120 project proposals were received out of which 57 were funded through the Dil Say Pakistan Social Innovators initiative. The executed projects included the following efforts (as cited in the Dil Say Pakistan Quarterly Report):

A Christmas Wish Wall—With an aim of celebrating Pakistan's diversity and bringing communities together, a Christmas Wish Wall was made by the Dil Say Pakistan Social Innovators to celebrate the shared joy of the Christian community of Pakistan.

A Holi Celebration—With the spirit of interfaith harmony and inclusiveness Dil Say Pakistan Social Innovators from the Hindu Community organized Holi in Lahore where a large number of people from Hindu, Muslim, Christian and Sikh community participated.

A Graffiti Project—Pakistani poet, Sara Shagufta's Urdu poetry is an expression of agency. She was abused, emotionally and sexually, in childhood, divorced by four men, shunned by her children, ostracized from the mushaira circle. Her life, commitment, and vision inspired a mural themed project that emerged as an outcome of one Dil Say Pakistan civic imagination workshop. The mural (which still exists at the time of writing) highlighted both the challenges women in Pakistan face and the power of vision as expressed through poetry.

While they were diverse in scope and focus, the proposals submitted all represented tangible, real steps towards the future of Pakistan envisioned through the workshops. They all also contributed to the overall presence of the Dil Say Pakistan campaign.

## Extending the Relevance of the Civic Imagination

Our partnership with the Dil Say Pakistan HIVE team confirmed that our approaches to the civic imagination could inform and support initiatives outside the United States. We also started to outline and model how such collaborations could operate, clearly delineating the strengths and limits of our expertise. Since then, we have been invited to take our work to other communities internationally—including those in Lebanon, Sweden and Austria—which has allowed us to further clarify how the civic imagination can be adapted, applied, and localized.

## Bibliography

Basit, Abdul. 2015. "Countering Violent Extremism: Evaluating Pakistan's Counter-Radicalization and De-radicalization Initiatives". *IPRI Journal* XV(2) (Summer 2015): 44–68.

Mirahmadi, Hedieh, Waleed Ziad, Mehreen Farooq, and Robert Lamb. 2016. "Empowering Pakistan's Civil Society to Counter Violent Extremism". *Contemporary Readings in Law and Social Justice* 8(1): 188–214.

Orakzai, Saira Mano. 2017. "Pakistan's Approach to Countering Violent Extremism (CVE): Reframing the Policy Framework for Peacebuilding and Development Strategies". *Studies in Conflict & Terrorism*. 10.1080/1057610X.2017.1415786.

Winter, Charlie. 2015. *The Virtual 'Caliphate': Understanding Islamic State's Propaganda Strategy*. London: Quilliam.

# CHAPTER NINE

# Imagination in the Classroom—New Media for Social Change

## KEY INSIGHTS

Over the past several years, we have offered an undergraduate course at the University of Southern California called "New Media for Social Change." Though it has evolved, the syllabus has always been premised on the civic imagination as a key pedagogical component of designing interventions for social change. Introducing civic imagination into our own university teaching allowed us to approach new media for social change creatively and through this support students in their own exploration of the possibilities and constraints associated with such practices. Experiencing civic imagination workshops early in the semester supported students as they connected with each other. Over the course of the semester, students surfaced case studies of existing campaigns and used these as inspiration to develop their own campaigns and workshops. The acquired critical and creative design skills enhanced their ability to deploy the civic imagination as an applicable and translatable tool.

## Introduction

The "pointy things" had seemed to pop up all over the university campus almost overnight. Most people passed them by with barely a notice, but for one group of our students they became a focus of intense ire that would inspire one of the most intriguing and productive social change campaign projects to come out of our experiences teaching undergrads. Over the past several years, we have offered a course at The University of Southern California called "New Media for Social Change." Though the syllabus has evolved a bit from year to year, the culminating project has generally been a comprehensive plan for a multi stage media rich social change campaign. The "pointy things" campaign arose from one group of students finding that they shared a sense of outrage about the recent proliferation on campus of what they considered to be a waste of University funds; a recurring architectural element made of brick and stone, about ten feet high and capped with a pyramidal point, hence the group's moniker. As far as the students were concerned, the pointy things served no purpose other than to convert tuition dollars into eyesores. They leveraged their gripe into a compelling project. They investigated the role of student input and governance in terms of University financial decision-making and designed a campaign to raise awareness and participation amongst the student body at large. They created a digital game based around the creation of memes. They interviewed members of the undergraduate student government. They also learned about how their university works, gained a sense of agency, and had fun working together as a team.

## Workshops Building Teams

This last point about enjoyable team work is actually one of the more important takeaways from the anecdote. We believe that the integration of our civic imagination workshops into the classroom activities was an important part of how this team formed an effective internal dynamic. In this chapter we reflect on how civic imagination created opportunities for empowerment, empathy and action oriented skill development within an undergraduate higher education context. And also how the classroom served as another important site for us to develop, test, and refine our tool kit of civic imagination workshops.

Since we began offering the course in 2014, we have always taken an approach that combines theory and practice (a hallmark of the Media Arts + Practice division in the School of Cinematic Arts where the course resides). We introduce students to the literature on participatory politics as well as relevant research methodologies. Students complete case studies on organizations or campaigns that leverage new and social media in interesting ways for social, civic or political action employing techniques such as media analysis, ethnographic observation and literature review. We have also always integrated our civic imagination workshops into the class in various ways.

The most common way has been to run a session early in the semester with the entire class participating in the world building workshop complete with brainstorm, story composition, performance and reflection. We have also run the remix workshop in a similar way. The students have consistently found this to be a rewarding experience. As in other contexts where we've run these workshops, students appreciated the novelty of the creative and fun approach that also allowed them to identify real world concerns and values and to connect with each other in meaningful ways. Over the course of several different semesters we further integrated the workshops in diverse ways.

## Imagination in the Curriculum

One semester we made workshop creation a key activity of the course. We trained the students in workshop facilitation and had them practice running workshops with each other. Then, working in small groups they developed workshops of their own through an iterative process of designing, testing and refining. There were some impressive outcomes from this process including workshops focused on design thinking, impactful storytelling, guerilla libraries and interaction design. Along with these specific skill areas, each workshop focused on applying those skills towards social issues and civic engagement. Several of these student-designed workshops live on and can be accessed on the byanymedia.net website.

More recently, we have oriented the course to focus student efforts on larger plans for multistage social action campaigns. In this context we still retain the workshops as an important element of student learning. Rather than having students design novel workshops, we have them prepare and run existing workshops either with their fellow classmates or outside groups. This preparation focuses on gaining a deep understanding and familiarity with the various stages, activities and concepts of the workshop in question, as well as an emphasis on facilitator training. For many of our students, this has been a novel and rewarding experience. It gives them a chance to step into a leadership role and practice public speaking and self-confidence. It takes a lot of confidence to get up in front of a group of people and ask them to follow your directions for the course of a workshop that might run for several hours. To be successful, students have to be able to manage their time efficiently, work well as a team, empathize with and listen to their participants and be able to adapt to changing situations and input on the fly.

Adaptability and empathy were particularly important in some of the first civic imagination workshops our students ran since their participants were elementary students; younger participants will definitely keep you on your toes. The elementary students were involved in a campus-based leadership academy at USC called Penny Harvest (previously mentioned in the introduction of our book). Our partnership with Penny Harvest was particularly apt since the program was focused on inspiring young people to think of themselves as future leaders in their communities and to help equip them with the skills to become such. Our students ran the Remixing Stories workshop with the Penny Harvest young folk. A few of our students had some experience working with youth, but for most it was their first time stepping into a role like that where they became the teachers. Several of our students talked to us afterwards about what a meaningful experience it had been for them. The primary goal had been to support a creative experience for the elementary students in which they could share stories and articulate social values and enhance their sense of agency, and our college-aged students got a similar boost to their own sense of agency and potential to serve as mentors and leaders in the future.

In the most recent iteration of our course, our students ran civic imagination workshops with each other. This gave us a chance to test out some of the newest workshops we've been developing for this book. We observed our students running and participating in these workshops but did not intervene as they unfolded. We started with the Monuments from the Future workshop in which participants examine public spaces as sites of potential civic action, imagination and intervention. We had already seen previous examples of how students could get passionate about exerting agency over the shared space of the campus in the 'pointy things' project described at the beginning of this chapter. This workshop is our attempt to enhance opportunities for that kind of exploration and to really bring an element of imagination to the experience. It is also a workshop in which the main creative activity is focused on material construction rather than narrative creation. We ask participants to use basic arts and crafts materials to mock up and deploy a 'monument from the future' as a way of bringing a physical manifestation of an imaginary future into real world public spaces where others will be able to see and experience this imaginative object.

Our students had a restricted amount of time to run these workshops; only about half of the recommended three hours. By dint of this necessity they had to make adaptations and adjustments to the workshop flow. This is a great reminder to any potential workshop facilitators that our instructions can always be seen as a starting place and a blueprint for an experience that can be molded to meet the needs and constraints of a given context. In the case of the students running the 'monuments' workshop this meant that they chose to drop elements of the workshop that focus on using pop culture touchstones to seed and then flesh out a narrative of the future that then inspires the material construction of the monument and its intervention in a public space. They focused their time on making observations of public spaces around campus and then designing, building and deploying imaginative futuristic objects that would alter those places in positive ways for the people inhabiting them.

These constructions included a synthetic solar powered (and power producing) tree and a shimmering art installation/chill out space called 'Welcome Home.' Mind you, these were small, tabletop sized constructions made from cardboard, construction paper and sundry little items at hand. But they represented big ideas. What's more, the act of building tangible objects together in that way gave a form to those ideas in a way that profoundly influenced their development and expression. Not only was it fun and engaging for students to make things with their hands, it opened up different pathways to creative thinking. It was also a visible reminder to students that their own habits of thought and action can benefit from occasional shake-ups. This is a core theme of our civic imagination workshops in general and nicely highlighted in this particular case, as confirmed by student reflections discussed below.

The group that created the 'Welcome Home' construction had chosen a nearby intersection as their space for observation and intervention. The intersection marks the border of campus as it interfaces with the surrounding residential neighborhood. It is a major thoroughfare in terms of foot traffic. The students had observed that despite so many people sharing a space, there was no opportunity for connection or slowing down; everyone was on their way somewhere and largely set in the track of their own individual world. Their idea for 'Welcome Home' was to create a structure that could be built near the intersection that would be large and airy and mostly open directly to the sidewalk, but that would allow passerby to easily step inside to see what was going on within. There would be sparkling reflective surfaces to catch the eye and entice folk to slow down and check it out. Once inside, there would be cozy places to sit and take a break from the daily routine. There would also be spaces for interactive digital artworks that would change periodically and invite participation and response from the community. Their idea was to make a space that would make interstitial public spaces feel potentially more homey, and to invite interaction and reflection between people who occupy the same geography but rarely get a chance to interact. These interactions could be face to face in real time, or else mediated through the digital artworks which would collect responses and input from users and integrate them into the art in a way that would allow it to change overtime to reflect the people who had been there.

The students running this workshop also chose to make it a 'surprise twist' that their participants were actually going to place their constructions in the places for which they had been designed. The students very much enjoyed this aspect. The 'Welcome Home' group took their construction (basically an open-fronted box with shiny decorations) and used yarn to hang it from the arm of a crosswalk signal at their intersection. They then stood back and observed people passing by to see what they might make of their colorful object popping up in this unexpected place. Their sense of playful intervention was energizing. They were not even overly disappointed when their object elicited barely a glance or reaction for the various passerby. They mainly felt affirmed in their sense of the spaces tendency to reinforce social alienation and their new sense of interest and agency in ideas around shaking up such tendencies.

The group that made the solar powered tree had a similar experience. Their design took a more fanciful futuristic approach more in line with the original intent of the workshop. They imagined an enormous tree that is a hybrid of synthetic and organic components that harnesses the sun in both traditional and novel ways. Not only does it perform photosynthesis, it incorporates photovoltaic elements to drive its electronic components and pass along that power to other people. In the simplest form, the tree allows folk to charge their electronic devices. But it also serves as an inviting home for wildlife that is otherwise missing from its intended site of installation at the USC Village.

The Village is a recent, massive expansion of the university's footprint. Though USC owned the land for a long time, its previous use had been for mainly small, locally owned shops and restaurants. With the development of the Village, high rise student housing towers were constructed and mostly national chain stores and restaurants moved in along with more high end local fare. It represented a huge disruption of the local landscape, eliciting mixed feelings in the community. The students imagined their hybrid tree as an attempt to create a more welcoming, natural aspect to the space. In addition to providing shelter for wildlife and power for people, the tree would play pleasing music beneath its massive boughs and provide delicious fruit, free for the picking.

The small scale mockup that the students made during the workshop lacked these functional qualities. Still, the students enjoyed the process of visiting the Village with a tangible manifestation of their vision in hand and temporarily installing it on the edge of a central fountain with a little bit of scotch tape to hold it in place. The intervention was totally non-destructive. And as with the Welcome Home project, the tree failed to gather much attention for the short duration of its life in the Village. But it still served as a locus of discussion and aspiration. It made tangible a sense of agency and delighted the students as they carried out their small act of creative subversion in a space that had previously seemed beyond their reach for intervention or interaction.

In its extended form, the workshop does include more ideas and instructions to help the constructed objects make a bigger impact on the spaces where they reside, including suggestions such as including explanatory signage or other visual cues that invite closer inspection and engagement from passerby. Still, upon reflection at the end of the workshop, students felt that there was real utility and opportunity in the experience for helping people envision, plan and activate agency over public spaces. They felt that it made them really consider the built environment and its impact on human action and interaction, and that it was something that they had not thought of with such clarity in the past.

Students also ran the Remixing Inspiring Stories workshop with each other during that class. We have discussed this workshop at length in other places in the book (as in Salzburg) so will spend less time recounting this iteration here. One of the interesting things about this session was an emphasis on children's stories in particular. Students enjoyed reminiscing about their favorite stories from when they were very young and getting to learn about each other and this distant phase of their past lives. Touchstone stories included, *"Are You My Mother?"*, Disney's *Tarzan* and *Beauty and the Beast*, *Avatar the Last Airbender* and the *Wiggles*. When they created their own stories there was a surprising degree of similarity in their narratives. Several were about anthropomorphized animals who experienced some sense of exclusion from their communities but made friends who helped them discover their unique talents and attributes, eventually leading to social acceptance. Characters included a dog with spikes named Stephanie, Brian the Goose and Deandre the Dog. During reflection, students equated these narratives with their own experiences struggling to fit in and find acceptance. They shared concerns about mental health, loneliness and the complicated relationship between issues like these and their experiences of social media and the tensions between carefully crafted appearances and reality as it is lived day to day.

## Pivoting Toward Projects

In both workshops students experienced something we have observed in various contexts—an opportunity to break out of the kinds of roles that they have come to inhabit by dint of routine or institutional structures. Even though they share classes and a campus, many of them shared with us that they almost never get a chance to connect with each other or their professors in ways that bring out these other aspects of their shared humanity. We've seen this with teachers, coworkers, activists, parishioners and so on; in contexts where people were just getting to know each other or else had known each other for a long time. And in this case, as in many others, the outcomes and goals of the workshop weren't the only aspect of the context in which these students came together, but they did create important opportunities for shared experiences, creative expression, exploration of values, and a deeper understanding of the future they were all facing and working towards together.

In our class, the workshops were an important pivot point towards the students' final projects. In these, they laid out detailed plans for large scale social interventions that would include innovative uses of new and social media. Some aspects of these planning projects can be found in the final workshop of this book, "Creating an Action Plan." Many of the action plans devised by our students focused on creating and facilitating real world experiences along with smart use of digital tools. The workshops gave them structured examples of how you might organize activities and the larger concept of civic imagination helped them to conceptualize diverse kinds of social interventions. Their final projects included the creation of a podcast that unpacked the complicated perspectives and truths behind controversial current and historical events as an intervention into the culture of 'fake news'; a fundraising program for homelessness resources centered around large scale sit down dinners for donors, providers and those experiencing homelessness; a photography based campaign to deconstruct and expand notions of beauty and body positivity; projects about food deserts, climate change research and more.

In the same way that we used the workshops as one tool and activity amongst many, in service of a larger goal, we hope that others will be able to adapt them to the specific needs and logics of their own contexts.

# CHAPTER TEN

# Of Two Faced Bunnies in the Woods—Brussels, Belgium

## KEY INSIGHTS

In 2018, we ran multiple civic imagination workshops to support the launch of a creative media initiative in Belgium. The beauty of our encounter with the team behind this particular effort was the fact that the project was so nascent. This offered us a great opportunity to think through how the civic imagination could support creative projects. Collaborating with the creative team helped us begin to transform civic imagination into a participatory tool that creatives could use to seed multi-faceted story worlds that support story generation, development, and circulation across multiple media channels.

## Introduction

"Batman does stuff and people don't know. And, that is inspiring," Melanie[1] explained as her group presented their inspiring stories during a Remixing Stories workshop in Brussels, Belgium. She also shared the other stories that her group

---

1. Pseudonyms used to protect participants' anonymity.

members had brought to the table, which included: Forrest Gump (because he faced personal challenges and social ostracism), the anime/manga character Naruto (who struggled against limitations others set on him), and an unpopular (yet sympathetic) female character in the latest season of Big Brother. To this group, made up of young people from a socially marginalized neighborhood in Brussels, these stories were all about people judging others at first sight. As one member of the group explained it, "judgement in this world is not enough, we first have to talk to each other." As facilitators, we acknowledged these insights as we always did during our workshops. We also made note of what the youth said on separate sheet titled "creative ideas" as this particular workshop sought to bring civic imagination to the early development of a creative project in Belgium.

Over the course of two weeks in May 2018, we ran multiple civic imagination workshops to help the creative team engage with community members and the stories that mattered to them so that these insights could inspire and inform the media making process. The experience offered us the unique opportunity to work with media makers at the start of a project and experiment with tapping the civic imagination as a tool for story generation, development, and circulation.

Funded by the US Department of State, our trip was facilitated by the US Embassy in Belgium whose staff served as key intermediaries in setting up the collaboration with the media makers and communities. From the beginning, we were very mindful of what this connection with the US government meant, particularly at this particular moment. In fact, we committed even more explicitly to the participatory dimensions of our work because of our concern about how our presence would be interpreted. We wanted to use the civic imagination as a framework that surfaces, but does not dictate, narratives and aspirations. Still, these considerations were continually present during our time in Brussels as we listened to all feedback we received throughout our stay.

As we soon understood, we were meeting the creative team—made up of a film director, a camera person and a screenwriter[2]—at a very nascent stage for the project. When the film director, the unofficial lead on the project, first described it to us, their narrative idea centered on a fictional young Belgian named Mohammad, who resides in Molenbeek, an immigrant-dominated and economically underserved area of Brussels. Frustrated with the limitations that his geography and identity impose on him and the judgment he faces as he moves through his life, he decides to transform himself into "Michel", a young Belgian man living in Woluwe, an affluent suburban commune in the city. The story, which the team initially saw unfolding as an episodic series, would then follow Mohammad/Michel

---

2. To protect the project, we have omitted the names of members of the creative team.

as he negotiates living a dual life and through it experiences just how complicated and grey (rather than black and white) the different worlds can be. As they were starting to tentatively think through the elements of the story, the creative team members were each in their own way interested in thinking through how their narrative could play out across various media platforms. They were also very interested in finding ways to work with local communities to source, workshop and possibly co-develop material.

Though they had some history of working together in various configurations, the media makers actually did not know each other that well. Through our early conversations, we started to define our role as facilitators who bring a civic imagination approach to the team as they define their roles and articulate the project's scope, shape, and goals. In particular, we stressed that our rootedness in participatory culture and the participatory practices associated with such communities supported an approach grounded in grassroots community. We saw a real possibility here to have our approach influence key aspects of this project.

In the end, we ran seven civic imagination workshops with communities in Belgium (in Brussels, Mechelen and Antwerp), engaged with the local areas relevant to the project, and continued to discuss all aspects of the project with the creative team throughout our time there. Our workshop participants included high school students involved with nonprofits in Brussels and Antwerp, college students in a communications program, employees of TARMAC, a hip-hop centered public television channel targeting youth, and US embassy employees. Though we facilitated most of the sessions, the role played by the creative team increased gradually, to the point where they co-facilitated our final session with us.

Working with the team in Brussels presented us with an opportunity to see our workshops as tools that support the creation of a media project. Observing the process, we learned that the practices we associate with the civic imagination help media makers in many ways. Experiencing the workshops personally can help the creative team coalesce. Running worshops with concerned communities helps them understand their characters and audiences. Community connections can lead to partnerships that can eventually support distribution and circulation as well.

## Connecting the Creative Team

We decided that our first workshop would be with the media makers themselves. We started this workshop by asking them to share a description of a memory object with all of us. We then asked them to narrate the story they linked with their chosen object. Immediately, the conversation become more substantive and personal. One team member shared a particularly poignant story about baby shoes he got from his grandfather in Algeria. He recounted that he was wearing the shoes when he landed in Belgium, and now they reminded him of his childhood in Algeria even though he hasn't been able to travel there in more than eight years. Another member shared photographs of scenery that remind him of his parents and the times he associates with them. The third team member described a bracelet her dad gave her as a teenager that she hated. She thought it was so ugly and not at all her style, but later she realized that he gave it to her because of its message to follow her dreams. We used these objects as the entry point into the "Origin Stories" workshop where each person imagined a magical or powerful special tool based on their memory object. The results were a magic bracelet that helps you let go of your fears, images that help you see your dreams and magic shoes that take you back in time. We then asked each team member to create an origin story that would connect this magical object to them. As the team shared, they learned about each other and started to build a more supportive rapport around their project as well.

## Imagining Place—About Brussels and Belgium

Our ongoing conversations with the team alerted us to the specific considerations that Belgium and Brussels introduced to the project. While the Brussels bombings of 2016—when the airport and train station in Brussels were bombed—certainly loomed large, it was really the social, cultural, and economic divisions within Brussels and the search for a cohesive Belgian identity that surfaced as a recurring, and central, theme. To help us navigate these realities, the team took us on walking tours of Woluwe and Molenbeek, two Brussels communes (districts) with layered experiences and imagined cultural, social and economic profiles that brought to life the everyday divisions that permeate Belgian life. Their idea for the Mohammad/Michel story grew out of their desire to reimagine these realities. Through these conversations, we quickly realized our civic imagination related efforts on this project needed to engage with imagination and place.

The divisions that the team described are supported by scholarship that engages themes centered on Brussels and Belgium. Scholars Christian Kesteloot and Pieter Saey define Brussels as both a "highly successful metropolis" and "a divided city" with "Belgians and EU citizens mainly living in the Outer City, and the poor non-EU citizens mainly living in the Inner City." As Kesteloot and Saey further note, the city's poorer non-EU inhabitants are generally "culturally voiceless" resulting in what these scholars see as a "socially unstable" situation (Kesteloot and Saey 2002, 60–61).

These divisions are further complicated by Flemish and French language barriers, which bilingualism scholar Baetens Beardmore (2010), writing a decade ago, noted make language "the most explosive force in Belgian political life." As we learned, Flemish and French language preferences are truly divisive in Belgium. Language was one of the defining characteristics that people used to identify themselves as belonging geographically, culturally, and socially. Having grown up in francophone parts of Brussels, two members of the team only spoke French. Only the camera person was fluent in both Flemish and French. All of them spoke English.

The members of the creative team explained that their fictional protagonist Mohammad/Michel was only able to move between Molenbeek and Woluwe because he was fully fluent in Flemish and French. Though they continued to explore how he would perfect his transformation using clothes, make-up or even magic, his language skills, were, in fact, his Belgian super power.

Because "being Belgian" and moving past the divisions that define Belgian life was so important to the project, we decided to include questions around the future of Belgian and European identity in our workshops with youth. Though they varied some, the young people's aspirations for Belgium in 2060 centered around a vision in which Belgium's diversity would be recognized as its key defining characteristic. Words like "multicultural", "multilingual", "borderless", "united", "complex" appeared repeatedly. Though there was some overlap, visions for the future of Europe focused more on finding a unifying, but still empathetic, identity as words like "equality", "unity", "open minded" and "diversity" surfaced. We discussed these patterns with the media makers so they could start to identify how their story could connect with existing conversations around Belgian and European identities. These conversations suggested prompts that the project could use to encourage dialogue around this topic.

## Mapping Story Terrains

The young people we met through our workshops provided us with many popular culture stories that inspired them. These included shows and films (like *Snow Piercer*, *Black Panther*, *Mad Max*, *Black Mirror*), prominent figures (like Carrie Fisher, and Martin Luther King) and enduring texts (like the Bible). Though it was too early to make any conclusions about how and why these stories resonated with our participants, we saw how collecting such inspiring stories could help identify recurring themes (struggle against a formidable force, overcoming expectations), characters (individual heroes and hero collectives), and plot elements that resonated with members of these communities.

We also got a glimpse of how our workshop methodology could surface themes, challenges and aspirations specific to particular communities. Mapping these story 'terrains' helped the project team as they continued to develop their storyworld and communities that Mohammad/Michel would inhabit.

The potential for civic imagination as a creative tool was most clearly demonstrated through two workshops we ran back to back with very different communities. In the first of the two workshops, we worked with college students at the Thomas More Hogeschool in Mechelen. For them, remixing inspiring stories brought up coming of age narratives. Iconically, one group created the "Two Faced Bunny in the Woods" remixed story in which Ernest, a traumatized bunny, is abandoned by his family. He:

> ...is devastated and decides to get drunk and do drugs and forget about it all. He ends up tripping so bad he thinks he was in the land of the dead. After exploring the land of the dead for a while, Ernesto decides it was time to go home. When he reaches the bridge, however, he is greeted by a friendly bunny—Mimi. When he walks towards her, Ernesto wakes up from him drug induced dream.

A coming of age narrative, this story was about realizing that it is ok to need help. Like their classmates at this Hogeschool, members of this group were very focused on the issues they were dealing with as young adults.

A few hours later, we almost experienced culture shock when we ran the same workshop with high school and early college-aged youth affiliated with Let's Go Urban, a non-profit offering after-school interest based programs to youth in the city of Antwerp. Most of these youth had arrived in Belgium recently; many of them had an immediate migration memory. And the stories they shared focused on migration as well. In one story, migrants from Vietnam, Norway and Morocco travel to Belgium and meet in a Flemish language course. They become friends. One day they decide to take a boat ride together, and for the first time they are all happy.

Though migration was clearly a key theme for these young people, their stories also touched on other topics, more closely related to the coming of age narratives we had just experienced in Mechelen. But, in Antwerp, these stories centered parental expectations, life aspirations, and self acceptance. In one such story, we met Robin, a 16 year-old boy who was not doing well in school. All he wanted to do was dance. His father tried to pressure him to work harder in school and did not support his love of dance. His mother was more sympathetic and wanted to support him in what he wanted to do. Robin's parents fought over this and eventually split up. Robin lied to his dad and started to take dance classes. He was so happy dancing that he started to do better in school. A few years later, when he was 22, he realized that "nothing is going to be fine, it's going to be ok". He accepted himself as he was.

In another group's story we met a young man who was the "King of Karate". Still he felt unfulfilled, like something was missing in his life. Then, he started to give classes and realized that it's all "about the people around him". He changed his life and focused on his students and so he realized that it is the real connections with others that made him whole.

As we reflected on these two workshops with the project team, we discussed how understanding youth in these two communities, their starkly different life experiences, and the stories they told could help them develop their creative project. The director noted that the stories he had been hearing shaping his vision for Mohammad/Michel as the central character. They were also helped him visualize the world which he would inhabit. Meeting the young people had also inspired him to think about how community participation could support the development of this project. We got a strong sense that the communities we encountered wanted to participate. They wanted to share their stories and experiences. As a group of high school participants told us after one of our workshops, we were the first people to ask them to talk through their hopes for the future and the stories that mattered to them.

## Connecting with Communities

The "Infinite Hope" and "Remixing Stories" workshops generated stories and insights that could be helpful to the team as they fleshed out their Mohammad/Michel narrative. They also connected the creative team with communities that could become part of the project as it moved forward. Such connections had the potential of greatly expanding the participatory possibilities of how the project came to life.

Though we left before the project was actually realized, our experiences with the creative team in Belgium helped us articulate a clearer vision for the civic imagination as a participatory creative media making tool.

## Bibliography

Beardsmore, H. Baetens. 2010. "Bilingualism in Belgium". *Journal of Multilingual & Multicultural Development* 1(2): 145–154. 10.1080/01434632.1980.9994007.

Kesteloot, Christian and Pieter Saey. 2002. "Brussels: A Truncated Metropolis". *GeoJournal* 58(1): 53–63. https://www.jstor.org/stable/41147731

# THE PRACTICE GUIDEBOOK

Now the action really gets going. In this section, we share detailed instructions for our six civic imagination workshops. Whether you've read the preceding chronicles of how we developed this approach, or whether you're just going to dive right into to doing it yourself, we have made every effort to provide all the tools, context and guidance you'll need to successfully facilitate any, or all, of these workshop plans. To this end, we also include some general facilitator tips below.

In our experiences, we have seen these workshops to be beneficial in all kinds of different contexts, from team building and development to education and activism. If you've found your way to this book, it's likely that you already have a context in mind where you think that civic imagination practice will provide some kind of boost. With a little bit of creativity and forethought we believe these workshops can be adapted and integrated to almost any kind of purpose. Though we provide and suggest as much detail as possible, we hope you will also feel empowered to use these instructions as a jumping off place from which to launch your own ideas and implementations.

# CHAPTER ELEVEN

# General Notes About Facilitation

We recognize that each facilitator develops their own style and respect these individual choices. With that in mind, we suggest that the following general notes can be integrated into various facilitator approaches to support workshop flow:

- **Be curious about your participants.** Try to learn as much as you can about your participants as this will help you better understand where they are coming from. If you are working with a community host/coordinator, ask many questions in the workshop planning phase. During the session, be attentive to what participants share with you, regardless of whether it is related to the workshop or not.
- **Establish ground rules for participation and invite everyone to participate.** It is important that participants understand that their participation matters and that you will be offering multiple ways to participate. The goal is to create a friendly, relaxed environment rooted in mutual respect so that creativity can flow.
- **Create context.** Make sure participants have a strong sense of the intentions and goals of the workshop as well as a general sense of the overall structure and flow. Knowing the general road map will help them relax and build trust.

- **Use accessible, easy to follow language.** Break down complicated terms and concepts so they are easier to grasp. Don't hide behind complex expressions.
- **Define key terms.** Be sure to provide definitions for all key terms you are using so that all participants can follow what you are saying.
- **Stress that all contributions matter.** There are not right or wrong answers. Participants need to feel confident about speaking up.
- **Give time warnings for various sections.** You are the time keeper. Participants should focus on doing the workshop (and not watch the clock).
- **Leave breathing time.** Do not be afraid of silences during brainstorms.
- **Let participants lead you.** Try to not let your preconceived ideas about how things should go dictate how things turn out. We set up guidelines and creative constraints to support creativity, not stifle it.
- **Be flexible and adapt the workshop to the needs and abilities of your participants.** Sometimes your participants will take the workshop in an unexpected direction. Accept this and be ready to accommodate them. There is always a reason, try to understand where they are coming from.
- **Be honest.** Be ready to share something about yourself. Consider what this might be beforehand. Participants need to understand who you are and why you are running this workshop.
- **Plan and practice.** Make sure you prepare to run the workshop. Know how long it will take and what you'll be doing as a facilitator. Plan for the transitions between activities. How will you keep time? How will responsibilities be divided amongst multiple facilitators? If it is your first time running a particular workshop, doing a practice run-through with a small group of friendly volunteers is a great idea.
- **Be open to surprises.** Unexpected things could happen and you need to anticipate as this as much as possible. Some of the workshops invite people to do things that may be a little outside their comfort zone and they may react to in various ways. Be supportive as they navigate their uncertainties. Also, recognize that they may be bumping up against limits of what they can do.

# CHAPTER TWELVE

# Workshop: Origin Stories—Imagining Ourselves as Civic Agents

*We connect the imagination to personal and social identities and the ways people think about their own capacities for social action.*

## Overview/Intro/Core Idea

This activity can be run as a workshop or completed as an individual process of reflection and creative writing. Much of the civic imagination is about looking forward and shaping a vision of the future. An important starting place for this work is often in our own pasts.

In this activity, participants are guided to identify a Memory Object; something tangible and personally evocative from another time and place in their lives. It might be something that was transient or permanent, something they still have with them or that was lost. The key is that it becomes a totem of memory, opening up a connection between the world of yesterday and of today. After an object has been identified and described, participants work individually or in groups to begin an analysis of these rich and evocative objects, identifying how they connect to themes such as sentimentality, nostalgia, family, community, labor, loss and so forth. This work helps people connect with parts of themselves that they do not

Fig. 12.1 Origin stories. Image Credit: Greg Whicker

always conjure or bring forth in the daily flows of their lives and public identities. It gives people a chance to get to know each other in new ways, and sets them up to enter a reflective, receptive and creative mode that is conducive to the work ahead.

Participants then use their memory objects to fashion origin stories from their own pasts. This creative exercise draws on traditions of superhero and fantasy fiction. Participants can either imagine themselves as characters in their own stories or create a new fictional cast. The goal is to create a narrative where the memory object plays an important role and becomes an emblem of or vehicle for a special power or skill. This power or skill is wielded to bring about change that is meaningful for the participants. Stories are then collected and shared, providing material for further reflection and feedback amongst participants in group settings.

Sharing memory objects and their stories with each other creates a degree of intimacy and vulnerability among the workshop participants; it enables trust as people talk about stuff that is at the core of our common humanity. This intimacy can them be used as the starting point for many creative and civic endeavors.

## Logistics/Nuts and Bolts

*Goal:* Skills developed in this workshop include understanding and deepening agency, self-assessment, expression, and creative writing. The workshop gets the imagination flowing in a personally meaningful way.

*Participants*: Participants need to be able to write (or otherwise document) their memory object narrative. We recommend that no more than 12–15 participants take part in a single workshop session.

*Duration:* The duration of the workshop depends on the number of participants. With approximately 12 participants, it will last 2 hours.

*Materials needed:* Pencils, paper, white board, flip charts, tables chairs—extension activities may require additional technologies.

*Space requirements*: The space should support individual writing exercises as well as group discussion.

*Preparation* (what the facilitator should do to prepare): The facilitator should be prepared to share their own memories to help start the discussion. The choice of memory object is important as it would help build connections with participants. Ideally, the facilitator should choose a memory object that touches on themes or notions that are likely to resonate with participants.

## Running the Workshop

### Icebreaker (15 Minutes)

To introduce workshop participants to each other, ask them to say their name and share something about its meaning or a meaning they associate with it. Use this to introduce the notion of the past memories and the stories we connect to them.

### Introduction (10 Minutes)

Introduce participants to the scope of the workshop. Explain that this workshop engages memory objects. These are objects that remind us of something personally important in our past that still influences us today and may even influence how we think about the future. Working with memory objects will help us reflect on our traditions, on things we cherish and want to carry with us as we move forward.

## SUGGESTED FACILITATOR MODIFICATION

One facilitator who ran this workshop wanted to more explicitly tease out the connections to memory and cultural identity in her particular community context. To support this, she opened the icebreaker by reading a poem by Lois Red Elk to highlight her own origins and help the participants connect to how unusual her traditional Lakota experience might be in mainstream western society.

## Activity Series

### Identify a Memory Object (15 Minutes)

Ask participants to think of a memory object that reminds them of a moment or time in their lives. This object could be something they still treasure; it may be something they no longer have in their possession. It could represent a moment that passed or a time that endured. Just ask that the object be evocative and builds a connection between the past and present.

Here is a possible prompt for this:

> We want everyone to bring their full selves to this session. To help us get to know each other, please tell us about a memory object, something from your past that is still relevant to you today. This may be something that you still have. It may be something that you lost or gave away along the way.
> Describe the object.
> Tell us how it entered your life.
> Share why it still matters to you today.

Ask the participants to respond to this prompt by jotting down a few notes or bullet points. If a pre-workshop assignment is possible, you may want to ask the participants to bring the memory object or a picture of it with them. If there is a need to cut down on the duration of the workshop, participants may be invited to respond to the above listed prompt ahead of the workshop as well.

## SUGGESTED FACILITATOR MODIFICATION

One past workshop facilitator noted it was sometimes difficult for participants to come up with a memory object that they feel connects to them. To help participants, she made the following amendment to this Part 1 of this workshop:

> *"I printed out images of approximately 50 memory objects from the 60s, 70s, 80s, and 90s. I cut them out as cards and spread them across the table. I allowed participants to select an object that jogged a memory. If they did not find an object that resonated with them, I told them they could choose an object that they still have or had that embodied sentimental meaning. Everyone ended up selecting and connecting a memory to objects that they found and wanted to grab more than one memory object out of the card pile."*

## Share Memory Objects and Identify Connections (15 Minutes)

Ask each participant to share their memory object working in pairs or smaller groups (of 2–3 participants per group). Request that other group members respond to the memory objects shared and reflect on how what is shared connects to themes such as sentimentality, nostalgia, family, community, labor, loss, and so forth.

## Craft Origin Stories (20 Minutes)

Participants then use their memory object prompt responses to fashion "origin stories" from their own pasts. Drawing on popular culture narratives, we define origin stories as the backstories of narratives that help explain how a character or group of characters emerged. For the purposes of this workshop, we are asking the participants to come up with origin stories (character narratives) that are connected to their chosen memory object. This creative writing exercise draws on traditions of superhero and fantasy fiction.

To launch this exercise, introduce the notion of origin stories by sharing examples of characters in well known narratives. These may include:

- Superman
- Black Panther
- Cinderella
- Harry Potter
- Never Ending Story
- Star Wars and so on

Participants can either imagine themselves as characters in their own stories or create a new fictional cast. The goal is to create a narrative where the memory object plays an important role and becomes an emblem of or vehicle for a special power or skill. This power or skill is then wielded to make something that is meaningful to the participant happen in the story.

If participants struggle to get started, we suggest that they return to the moment when they first encountered the memory object and what it meant to them then. They can then use this first encounter as the starting point as they develop their origin story and the objects' special power.

## Share Origin Stories (30 Minutes)

Ask each participant to share they origin story with the full group, by reading it out, or otherwise presenting it. They should connect their story to the memory object they selected.

Once all the origin stories have been shared, ask the participants to reflect and share their thoughts on the themes brought up the origin stories.

*Prompt: What themes do you notice in the origin stories shared?*

To help participants identify these themes, you may guide them to think closely about each story shared:

*Prompt*:

*Who were the characters?*

*What motivated them to act?*

*What power/strength did the memory object introduce to the narrative?*

*What difficulty did the characters have to overcome and how did they overcome it?*

*How did the story end? How could it continue?*

List the themes mentioned on a whiteboard or flipchart. Leave the list up on the board as a reference. Then ask each person to pass their origin story to the person next to them, so they are now working with someone else's memory object origin story. Participants can also choose to work on their own story if they prefer.

Ask each participant to review the origin story they received. Drawing on the themes it touches on, they should then identify how it might be used to generate a sense of connection between people.

*Prompt*:

*How could the origin story you received be used to generate a sense of connection between people who may otherwise see the world in different ways?*

*How could this be used to inspire people to view an issue of social or cultural relevance differently?*

Ask participants to use the piece of paper they received to jot down their responses to these questions.

Final Reflection (15 Minutes)

Invite a few of the participants to share their social theme responses with the larger group and use to this to transition to a broader discussion of how our memories and the stories we construct around them, can provide entry points into our histories and values. Lead a discussion about how memories can invite various forms of nostalgia and how these emotions can be both generative and destructive forces in our lives. End with a discussion of how these narratives can in turn help us find new ways to connect with each other and move towards building civically meaningful connections.

## Possible Extensions

The Origin Stories workshop lends itself to still image production and sharing on platforms such as Instagram and Facebook, and to creative writing publishing on platforms such as Google Docs, Medium and Wordpress.

# CHAPTER THIRTEEN

# Workshop: Infinite Hope—Imagining a Better World

*We recognize the value of utopian and dystopian narratives for helping people to think about what they are fighting for as well as what they are fighting against.*

## Overview/Intro/Core Idea

The "Infinite Hope—Imagining a Better World" workshop[1] is a future-focused workshop highlighting the power of stories as tools for fostering civic imagination and inspiring real world change. As this title suggests, the focus is on worldbuilding, that is, thinking about what alternative worlds might look like, reading them in relation to our own, and deploying them as a means of expressing and debating visions for what alternatives might be to current conditions. We find that alternative worlds free participants from the constraints on the imagination which are posed by a relentless focus on existing constraints which limit the possibilities for change.

---

1. An earlier version of this workshop was created by Gabriel Peters-Lazaro and Sangita Shresthova, along with Karl Bauman, Susu Attar, and Ilse Escobar.

Fig. 13.1 Infinite hope. Image Credit: Greg Whicker

The workshop leads participants through an exercise of building a future world in which both real and fantastical solutions to cultural, social and political challenges are possible, ultimately leading them to strategize how we may be able to get to this imagined future. The workshop begins with a big picture brainstorm. Working backwards, the participants then break into smaller groups to share insights and build on these imagined worlds to brainstorm character-based narratives of social change set in the shared future world. After working out their stories, the groups are then given a short amount of time to prepare a presentation of their narrative. Encouraging spontaneity, the final presentations invite participants to share their stories with others. This shared performative experience creates a sense of community and helps the group move toward reflection.

In effect, the workshop helps participants brainstorm the full range of possible and fantastical futures. Many of the political veterans in the organizations we work were initially skeptical of what they saw as the 'escapist' dimensions of our approach, but rethought this opposition when they saw how this approach opened new possibilities and re-energized participants.

## Logistics/Nuts and Bolts

*Goal:* This workshop offers a hands-on opportunity for participants to imagine how alternative narratives can inspire community building and participation to achieve systemic change. Supported skills include speculative design thinking, narrative construction, and critical thinking. Extension options then connect to participatory media making practices and related production skills.

*Participants:* Our own experience demonstrates that this workshop is well suited to a broad range of participants, including youth: mixed age groups, administrators, and media professionals. Ideally, this workshop is run with around 20–40 participants, though smaller and larger groups can be accommodated.

*Duration:* The basic workshop takes between 2 hours and 2 hours and 30 minutes, but can fluctuate depending on the number of participants and the debrief option you choose.

*Materials needed:* The materials needed for this workshop are:

- large flip charts/paper boards for brainstorm or whiteboard and markers
- sheets of paper and pencils to support group work
- props for performance (can include wigs, fabric, toys, anything, glue, paper, other crafting materials)

*Space requirements*: The workshop calls for space for a large group brainstorm (where everyone can see the whiteboard or large flip charts), space for small group work, and space for final performances.

*Preparation* (what the facilitator should do to prepare): Be ready to seed the brainstorm with initial brainstorm themes. We suggest preparing six in advance. You may draw on the list we provide or come up with your own. You may also bring along props for people to use in the final performance.

## Running the Workshop

### Icebreaker (15 Minutes)

As participants enter, hand them a card/print out that contains the following prompt:

> *Think of a story or character that inspires (or inspired) you to think about the future. This story or character could be based in a book, a film, a TV show, a song or any other popular culture narrative format.*

Ask them to write down their response on the sheet of paper you just handed them.

Once everyone arrives, go around the room and have everyone say their name and share the popular culture story/character that inspires them when they think about the future. Use the ice breaker to introduce fictional narratives and storytelling as a powerful tool that helps us express our experiences and connect with others.

---

## SUGGESTED FACILITATOR MODIFICATION

One facilitator who ran this workshop decided to share a short clip from the film *Back to the Future 2* as a way to jump start participants' exploration of how fictional stories can inform our visions of the future.

---

## Introduction (5 Minutes)

Introduce the concept of civic imagination as an approach that aims to open up possibilities, strengthen community, and express goals/dreams. Premised on the need to be able to imagine civic alternatives and possibilities to take constructive/creative action, the civic imagination can help guide action.

> **Civic Imagination defined:** "Before we can change the world, we have to be able to envision the possibility of change, we have to be able to imagine what kinds of change would be desirable, and we have to be able to think of ourselves as people capable of making change. This is what we are calling the civic imagination." (Henry Jenkins 2016)

> **World building defined:** Sometimes associated with science fiction, worldbuilding describes a process in which individuals or groups of individuals build imaginary universes. This approach flips traditional approaches to story making on its head as it supports the creation of a fictional world in which multiple narratives and elaborate backstories can thrive. It also provides mechanisms for many people to participate in the process of creating and elaborating on the world.

## Activity Series

### Future World Brainstorm (20 Minutes)

Use a board or flipchart. Building on your introduction, ask participants imagine a future aspirational world set in a specific year (i.e. 2060) where fantastical things are possible (this future is a fantasy). This is a future world where things are as they SHOULD and COULD be. We are NOT trying to predict how the world will be.

### Brainstorm Prompt

*In this workshop, we are going to collectively brainstorm a future world one based in the future. For the purposes of the brainstorm, we ask you to temporarily bracket your expectations of how this future world WILL be. Rather, we ask you to focus on how it COULD be, beyond realistic constraints. The fantastical is possible.*

Ask participants to brainstorm what the world looks like in terms of key themes, which may include:

*Food*
*Transportation*
*Education*
*Communication*
*Government*
*Travel*
*Health*
*Environment*
*Media*

We recommend that the facilitator seeds a few categories that are fairly neutral and appealing and then allows the participants to propose more once they understand the process. This will allow the facilitator to understand what the participants think of when they consider the future.

Do not worry if the brainstorm surfaces paradoxical, or even contradictory, future world visions. Resolving and bridging these contradictions will be supported through the story making process detailed in the next section.

If you feel that participants may hesitate to participate immediately in a free-wheeling brainstorm you may consider including interim steps to get the process started. One such step could include alternative brainstorm methods. You may choose to create the topics for the brainstorm and write them on a whiteboard one by one. Then pause, let people write ideas on post-it notes, place them on the board and then talk about them together. If you have a large number of participants, you may also use word cloud tools to support the brainstorm process.

### Story Making (20 Minutes)

Break participants into smaller groups of 4–6 participants and ask them to come up with a fictional story that happened between today and the year in which your world is set. The story should build on one of the themes fleshed out in the brainstorm and should help explain something that happened to move us towards the future world they have just created. To do this, have each group identify (and claim) one specific **sub-theme** of the brainstormed future world (i.e. sustainable floating pods as a **sub-theme** of housing). Ask each group to claim their sub-theme by circling it on the board you used for the brainstorm. This is, first and foremost, a story making activity.

The story the participant groups create needs to incorporate the following:

- a (human or other) character, group of characters, or a community
- a conflict (an issue that comes up in the story)
- a resolution to the conflict or a partial resolution is somehow reached through a series of narrative twists

Circulate and spend time with each group as they work on making their stories. If you see that a group is struggling try to help them by asking some of the following questions:

- Which of the areas included in the brainstorm resonated for you?
- Why do you care about these issues?
- What would need to happen between today and the world of the future to make this happen? Who might make this happen and why?
- What may be one step along the way?
- Who may take this step?
- Under what circumstances?
- What may they do? And how?
- What would this lead to?

## Performance Planning (15 Minutes)

Ask the participants to come up with a way to 'perform' the story back to the whole group. They should aim to make their improvised performance 1–2 minutes long (note: this guideline will result in a performance that takes around 5 minutes). Key elements of performance must include:

Some sort of action
Everyone in Group
Narration

Some of the participants may become anxious about the performance. Reassure them that such nervousness is normal and that we realize that they do not have enough time to rehearse and perfect their performance. In fact, the improvisational elements are key to the workshop process.

You may want to provide participants with assorted props to help them prepare for the performance. These could be anything you feel is appropriate and available to you.

*Performance!* (30 Minutes)

Each group shares back their story through a short performance. Allow each group to perform, but carefully calculate the time it will take to get through the performances as this will vary depending on the number of groups you have.

If you realize you are absolutely running out of time, you may choose to only have a few of the groups perform. This is not ideal as it undermines the community building aspect of the workshop, but it will still allow you to accomplish many of the workshop's goals.

As the facilitator keep careful track of the stories presented.

## Final Reflection (Ranges between 10 and 45 Minutes)

*Option 1—Short Reflection* (15 Minutes)

If time is of concern, you can move into a final reflection where you ask participants to consider the following questions:

- What did you notice in each story presented?
- What stood out to you?
- How did change occur?
- What may we be able to relate these observations to the way change occurs in the world around you?
- What did you notice about yourself, the other participants throughout this process?
- How can the imagination serve us in our civic lives?

Conclude the workshop with a personal reflection about how collective imagination can help us in our daily lives.

*Option 2—Iterative Group Reflection* (30–45 Minutes)

If you have more time, you can ask people to vote on three stories they want to discuss further. Alternately, you may check in with your colleagues to identify three stories without popular vote. If you do the latter, be sure to be transparent about the selection process.

Then ask participants to get up, move around and sit in a new place in the room. Ideally, you have them set up to be in groups of 4–6 people. The seating should be different from their previous group assignments. Identify one note-taker for each table. This note-taker will be designated for the duration of the small group reflection process. Then have the participants go through 3 rounds of discussion, each focusing on one of the three selected stories. Each round should last 12 minutes.

For each round have the groups answer the following questions:

- How does happens in the story? What changes between the beginning and the end?
- How does it reflect back to where we are today?
- What action might this story inspire? And what can you do as an individual? As a group?
- What is one thing we might be able to do when you leave here today?

Ask each note taker to share back from the discussions that took place at their table. And then open up the floor to a more general discussion.

End with a brief discussion of next steps. Next steps coming out of the workshop are very much up to the host organization. If the next steps are in flux, ask a few participants to share one thing they are taking away from the process that might influence something they will do in the next day or week. Thank everyone for participating before before adjourning.

## Possible Extensions

The outcomes of this workshop can be used to seed artistic projects that bring the imagined future worlds to life. For example, participants may collaborate to build artifacts from the future. They can also create storyboards to document their stories.

## Bibliography

Duncombe, Stephen. 2012. "Utopia is No Place" Open Field: Conversations on the Common (in conversation with Sarah Peters). August 27. https://walkerart.org/magazine/stephen-duncombe-utopia-open-field

Jenkins, Henry. Youth Voice, Media, and Political Engagement: Introducing the Core Concepts in *By Any Media Necessary The New Youth Activism*. New York: NYU Press.

# CHAPTER FOURTEEN

# Workshop: Step into the Looking Glass— Imagining Our Social Connections with a Larger Community

*We engage imagination inspired by popular culture as a fun way to connect with others through fictional characters, story-worlds and through this surface shared issues of concern.*

## Overview/Intro/Core Idea

The "Step into the Looking Glass" workshop invites participants to engage with well-known popular culture content worlds to build social connections and begin imagining community. Defined as the narrative universes contained in books, TV shows, movies, comic-books, and other popular culture or fan spaces, **content worlds** are used to surface cultural interests as an entry into a deeper exploration of shared values and connections.

The workshop is informed by fannish engagements with content worlds that draw on practices associated with participatory cultures, which Henry Jenkins et al. (2006) define as cultural practices that have "relatively low barriers" to entry, strong support to create and share content, and informal mentorship structures, participatory cultures are defined by members who "believe their contributions matter" and feel a "social connection" with each other as those with more experience mentor others. Crucially, participatory cultures allow individuals and communities to

Fig. 14.1. Step into the looking glass. Image Credit: Greg Whicker

contribute in whatever way they can and support a broad range of possible entry points into participation.

The "Step into the Looking Glass" workshop opens with a brainstorm to surface popular culture content that participants know and like. Participants then work in smaller groups based on their content world preference; each participant should be familiar with their group's selected content world. The facilitator invites each participant group to "enter their content world" by stepping through the metaphorical "looking glass" to engage with the imaginary world on the other side.

A series of prompts guide participants through a 'tour' of their chosen imaginary content world. Eventually, they imagine an encounter with a fictional character in this world. This character helps them 'discover' some surprising information that they can bring back to the "real world".

Once they resurface from their imaginary journey, each group shares what they saw and learned. The facilitator then has the groups swap stories so that another group can reflect on what other participants experienced and imagined. In this way, all the the participants engage with each other's stories through a process that taps participatory practices where everyone contributes, but no one fully controls a project.

## Logistics/Nuts and Bolts

*Goal:* The workshop surfaces practices that are crucial to imagining communities through popular culture content worlds and through this supports skills associated with fan based and networked activism.

*Participants:* This workshop is well suited for the following participants: young adults in community organizations, members of civic organizations looking to expand the cultural relevance of their work, high school students, and professional media organizations. The activities in this workshop allow participants to share their knowledge of popular culture. Well suited for groups of 10–30 participants.

*Duration:* The workshop runs for 2 hours, but can be completed in a shorter period of time with a smaller group of 16 or fewer participants.

*Materials needed:* Overall the technical requirements for this workshop are minimal as the workshop relies on a whiteboard, markers, paper, large sheets of paper, and colored pencils. The facilitator may consider creating a short media (video) piece as a part of the ice breaker and as an extension of the workshop.

*Space requirements:* Participants will be working individually and in groups. The workshop space should be conducive to both of these configurations.

*Preparation:* The facilitator will need to prepare an introduction to popular culture and content worlds including examples that resonate with their particular workshop participant group. The facilitator will also need to prepare the icebreaker cards to hand to participants as they enter the room.

## Running the Workshop

### Icebreaker (15 Minutes)

As participants arrive, prompt them to think of a popular culture entity, character, or location that they know. This can be something from their childhood or something they have engaged with more recently. This character or location could be tied to a film, a TV show, book, play or folk tale or other narrative they remember from when they were young(er). Ask the participants to write down the character's name or location on post-it card that they then put up on a board or wall.

After everyone has posted their card to the board, read each one aloud and ask the participant who contributed it to identify themselves (by name).

Ask the participants to then go up and collectively identify how the cards could be grouped together by theme, genre, type or any other organizing principle that makes sense. Possible organizational ideas could include (but should not be limited to):

Genre—comedy, mystery, etc.
Character specifics
Location similarities
Social themes

Conclude the ice breaker by asking the participants to collectively comment on what they noticed as they reviewed the cards. Leave the cards up and use them to jump start the workshop brainstorm described in the next section.

## Introduction (15 Minutes)

Cite some examples from the popular culture examples that the participants surfaced in the Icebreaker and introduce popular culture and content worlds as key concepts for the workshop.

Here are some basic definitions to use:

**popular culture** describes culture that is "ordinary" and has vernacular appeal. Though popular culture can often be seen as synonymous with commercially produced cultural products such as feature films and video games, it could also refer to more niche creations and folk traditions.

**content worlds** are the narrative universes contained in books, TV shows, movies, comic-books, and other popular culture or fan spaces.

## Activity Series

### Brainstorm (15 Minutes)

Building on the ice breaker, guide the participants through a brainstorm that surfaces content worlds that participants know and like. Start with having everyone write down 3 popular culture content worlds that come to mind. They can draw on the material surfaced during the Icebreaker.

**Prompt**
*Name 3 content worlds that resonate with you and that you know well.*

Then ask the participants to share their content worlds with the whole group. They should include a 1 sentence description of the world if it is one that may not be familiar to everyone. Write content world names on the board so they are visible to everyone, noting the ones that repeat more than once (with a circle or a plus sign next to it).

*Entering the World* (15 Minutes)

Allow participants to organize themselves into smaller groups (of 2–3 participants) based on content world preference; each participant should be familiar with their group's selected content world.

---

## SUGGESTED FACILITATOR MODIFICATION

One past facilitator experienced a challenge at this point as she had participants with significant age differences, which made it difficult for some of them to connect through shared content world affiliations. She explained that "When trying to create groups, some participants merged effortlessly with their content worlds, while a few were placed by preference and not their selections." To resolve this, she created some groups based on thematic similarities. They then mixed up these stories and content worlds to create a shared space for this workshop.

---

Once the groups are established, invite the participants to "enter their content world" by stepping through the metaphorical "looking glass." If you have space, you may actually create a improvised portal that everyone walks through. This can be a line on the floor or even two chairs with a space in between them. As they step through, ask the participants to imagine that they are able to literally enter their content world as they imagine it to exist. Use an example that you are familiar with to illustrate.

Use the following prompt to guide participants through a 'tour' of their chosen imaginary content world once they are in it:

*Touring Content World Prompt:*

*Imagine that you are on a tour of your content world. You are able to visit part of it that you would like to see. You are able to experience elements of it. You are able to able to speak to any character. The possibilities are endless. Based on your interests for this tour, answer the following 3 questions:*

1. *What is one location you would definitely want to see?*
2. *What would it be like to taste in this world? What would like to smell?*
3. *What would you like to experience?*

Visit each group to make sure all groups are able to immerse themselves in their world.

## Meet a Character (15 Minutes)

Once they have toured their world, ask participants to think of a character that they would like to meet during their content world tour:

*Prompt*:

*Identify a character or group of characters in this content world that you would like to meet. Who is it? Why would you want to meet them?*

Next, ask participants to imagine that this character, or group of characters, chooses to reveal some completely new information about themselves or the content world. This could be a narrative detail, background information, or a secret development that has never been shared with the world before. This information should be so significant that it changes the participants' understanding of the content world.

*Prompt*:

*What new information does the character share with you? Why does it matter? What does it change?*

Give the participants a heads up that they will be sharing their tour experiences and character insights with the rest of the group and give them a few minutes to prepare for this.

*Prompt*:

*Describe the content world that you toured*

*Introduce the character and explain their role in the content world*

*Share the information learned and why it is significant*

Make sure you identify partner groups before presenting (so groups know that they should pay careful attention to the presentation). Have each group present. The partner group should take notes or otherwise make note of important details.

*Connecting to the Real World* (20 Minutes)

Once everyone has presented, ask participants to swap stories (so the previously identified partner group receives another groups content world).

---

## SUGGESTED FACILITATOR MODIFICATION

Some facilitators skip the "swapping" step because participants are not sufficiently familiar with others' content worlds. In this variation of the workshop, each group just continues to work on their own content world for this part of the workshop.

---

Ask each receiving group to discuss the material they received, their perception of the character or groups of characters chosen and the information received. Then ask them to identify a real world topic that could be connected to the information revealed by the character (as described by the original group):

*Prompts*:

*How does this content world relate to the real world?*

*Why is the information learned significant?*

*What real world topic could it touch upon?*

Next, ask each group to imagine the information revealed by the character or group of characters could inspire us to take action on the topic they identified. They can assume that their audiences are somewhat familiar with this specific content world.

*Prompt*:

*If the character could come to our world, here today, what is one action they would want us to take based on what I just shared with you? How would they tell us take this action?*

*Make a Poster* (15 Minutes)

Using a piece of paper and colored pencils/markers, ask each receiving group to make a poster that shares the information revealed by the fictional character and connects this information to the real world topic they identified.

## Final Reflection (10 Minutes)

Have each group share the visual they created. Give participants a chance to respond. Finally, have the participants reflect back on the whole workshop to see what they learned about their engagement with popular culture.

> *Final Prompts*:
>
> *Let's return to popular culture, what do you notice about it now?*
>
> *How can engaging with popular culture help us connect with each other?*
>
> *How can popular culture worlds connect to the topics in the real world?*

# Bibliography

Jenkins, Henry et al. 2006. *Confronting the Challenges of Participatory Culture: Media Education for the 21st Century*, eds. D. John and . Catherine. Chicago: MacArthur Foundation.

# CHAPTER FIFTEEN

# Monuments from the Future—Bringing Imaginative Dimensions to Our Real World Spaces and Places

*We encourage an interplay between cultural geography, urban space, and the civic imagination.*

## Overview/Intro/Core Idea

This workshop is about making imagination tangible, shareable, and place-based. Many real world challenges that individuals and communities are struggling with can be situated within the logics of space and place. For example, issues like health, environment, education and so on can all be mapped onto local geographies as they connect with specific contexts and realities. Monuments from the Future is a simple, playful intervention that invites participants to construct fanciful place-based artifacts of the civic imagination from low cost materials, without a need for prior experience or skills in model making or fabrication.

The workshop begins with a simple place-based observation. Participants then work in groups to come up with some kind of intervention; maybe helping to unlock some underutilized potential of the space they observed or to bring something to the place that is currently lacking. Using materials available to them, they build artifacts that help re-imagine the space.

Fig. 15.1 Monuments from the future. Image Credit: Greg Whicker

## Logistics/Nuts and Bolts

*Goal:* This workshop helps people think creatively about the space around them. Starting with a location, we encourage participants to layer imagination over their surroundings to expand the possibilities of these real world spaces and places.

*Participants:* This workshop is best suited for people who are able to work in groups and independently. The workshop does include moments when participants leave the room, which needs to be considered in determining suitability. We recommend that the number of participants does not exceed 30.

*Duration options:* 2 hours (depending on number of participants)

*Materials needed:* Paper, pencils, crafting materials, glue, tape, string.

*Space requirements:* The workshop calls for a room that can support group work. Participants need to also have access to public or somewhat public spaces for the observation part of the workshop. Outdoor spaces are helpful for artifact creation.

*Preparation* (what the facilitator should do to prepare): The facilitator should ensure that the workshop space and nearby places are suitable for the workshop. They should also familiarize themselves with key issues facing the participant communities.

# Running the Workshop

## Icebreaker (15 Minutes)

As people arrive, ask them to think about a place they know, or have known in the past. This should be place that is meaningful to them. You may write the prompt on the board.

*Prompt*:

*Think of a place that you know or have known in the fast. This could be a town, a forest, a garden, any place. Visualize this place and recall why it is important to you today.*

Once all participants have arrived, go around the room and have people introduce themselves by briefly sharing the place they thought of in response to the prompt. As they share the memory of the place, ask the participants to elaborate on the feelings associated with it. Keep this brief, but give them a chance to share.

As people share, list the places mentioned on a whiteboard or flipchart. Use this list to introduce and connect place and imagination by stressing how the real and everyday places we encounter in our lives intersect with our imagination and connections with others. The meaning that these places take on in our lives changes over time. Note that spaces can encourage the imagination; they can also stifle it.

## Introduction (10 Minutes)

Drawing on the Icebreaker, introduce the notion of place to the participants and connect it to the imagination. Though the imagination may feel like an abstract concept it can, and needs to be, localized into particular places. Places anchor memories. Places serve as points of departure for many aspirations. Public places are also where our imaginations connect with others. We recommend that you also bring in a local example to demonstrate how a place can connect to the imagination. These examples could include statues, names of streets, parks, shopping malls, parking lots, hallways, and any other publicly accessible places you can think of.

## Activity Series

### *Place Based Observation* (20 Minutes)

Pair participants and ask them to identify a place nearby that they would like to observe for 10 minutes. They will work in pairs, but their observations should initially be carried out individually. Ask them to document what they notice. Once they identify a place, give them an exact timeframe and let them leave to carry out their observation.

*Observation prompt:*

*Work in pairs.*

*Choose a place to observe.*

*The place you choose should be publicly accessible and there should be human activity. It should be a place that is of interest to you and your partner.*

*Observe the scene for 10 minutes. You and your partner should observe from different vantage points and without conferring. Your goal should be discretion and non-interference. Ideally there will be a place for you to sit quietly on the periphery.*

*Make notes about:*

o *What you observe. This may include characteristics of the location—architecture, light, plant life, accessibility, sound, etc.*
o *Activities—who is there, what are they doing, do people interact, how so?*
o *Note how your observations shift over time*
 *After you finish your observation, jot down, or otherwise, record, your observations. Try to identify patterns in the activities and behaviors you saw.*
o *Did your observations raise any questions about your place? If so, what would be your strategy for answering them?*

*As you walk back to the workshop venue, briefly compare your observations with those of your partner—did you see the same things? Did you interpret them in the same way? Why do you feel this is the case?*

## SUGGESTED FACILITATOR MODIFICATION

Some of the facilitators have encountered situations where observing a place was not possible for various reasons (rural environments, access limitations). They came up with two ways to overcome this constraint that we offer here as possible options: 1. They conducted their observations online by examining available media (photos, videos etc.), or 2. They designated zones in the workshop space and asked participants to experience them and augment them. Both of these options call for additional planning on the part of the facilitator as access to the internet or additional set up time is needed.

*Identify Space/Place for Intervention* (15 Minutes)

Once all participants debrief and return, ask each group to share their observations with all the participants. Each share back should include a brief description of the place they observed, what they noticed, and what stood out to them. How does what they observe map onto their understanding of the history of this place? How does it connect to its current function?

Create a list of all the locations the participants observed on a whiteboard or flipchart. Once everyone has shared back, ask the group to review the list and identify which of the places inspire their imagination. Could they imagine changing that place in some way?

Give each participant 2 small post it cards (or a similar equivalent) with their name and ask them to 'vote' for two places that inspire their imagination the most—the ones they would like to change or rethink. Tally the votes and use these to create groups of 3–4 participants, each working on re-imagining one place.

### Inspire Place-Based Imagination (10 Minutes)

Each group should consider what their place could be in the future—what it can aspire to become? Can it support a certain experience? Can it trigger memories? Can it connect people? Whatever its quality or utility, each group needs to find something that they could bring to the place to make it more inspiring, imaginative, or otherwise meaningful. This should be an addition that facilitates a re-imagining of what the place means and how it functions. They should consider what this place has meant in the past and what it could mean in the future.

### Monument from the Future—Intervention (20 Minutes)

Creating a physical artifact makes the tangible connections between imagined and real spaces visible. The participants should use simple materials—cardboard, construction paper, staples, glue, yarn—to build their "monument from the future", an artifact, of their choosing that invites a re-imagining of the place they have selected. Ideally, the artifact the participants create would inspire and connect people somehow as they move through the identified place reflecting their aspirations for it. The participants should write a caption for their "monument" to explain what it is and how it functions. If possible, the monument should then be placed in the actual place so the workshop participants can view it there. If it is not possible to leave or install the artifact, then the participants should take a photo or otherwise document it and the intended location where it would have been placed.

### Touring (20 Minutes)

If possible, ask the participants to go on a tour to view all of the selected places and the created artifacts. Encourage them to document the monuments they created. Participants should also take the time to notice how the placed artifact is received.

Do people notice it? How do they react? Does the insertion of a "monument from the future" alter the meanings associated with that specific place? Why or why not? If touring is not possible, the participants can also take add photographs of their monuments and places to a photo collection that they can view together or individually.

## Final Reflection (10 Minutes)

After their real or virtual tour, participants return to the workshop venue for a final reflection. Invite all the participants to think back on the whole process by answering these questions:

What did they notice about the places included in the workshop?
How did creating a physical artifact affect their relationship with the place and other participants?
How do places acquire meanings?
How can we tap our imaginations to re-imagine the places around us?

Conclude the workshop by reflecting on how the places we inhabit influence us. They remind us of the past. They can also help us imagine yet unrealized possibilities.

# Possible Extensions

Beyond physical construction of the artifacts, this workshop can also be adapted to 3D modeling and printing as well as VR or AR applications. Physical models can be documented using the Google Street View app which has the ability to create photospheres that can be added to publicly viewable maps and experienced in VR viewers or on smartphones.

# CHAPTER SIXTEEN

# Remixing Stories— Forging Solidarity with Others with Different Experiences Than Our Own

*We propose that stories and imagining are crucial to networked connections made by disparate groups during struggles over social change and civic action.*

## Overview/Intro/Core Idea

Too often, our focus on contemporary problems makes it impossible to see beyond immediate constraints that confine our ability to bridge differences to build connections with people whose world views may be different from our own. Responding to this, the Remixing Stories workshop taps icons and narratives borrowed from popular culture to express civic identities and bridge divisions and differences that are making it hard for traditional political institutions to move forward with solving persistent problems. Participants begin by gathering and sharing stories that inspire them. Then, exploring each other's stories, they start to mix and recombine elements between stories, seeing how the combinations of unexpected elements lead to whole new creative narratives. As story remixing leads to real-life sharing, reflection, debate and collaboration, participants imagine how their combined stories might be enlarged and used to spark social movements and campaigns.

Fig. 16.1. Remixing stories. Image Credit: Greg Whicker

## Logistics/Nuts and Bolts

*Goal:* This workshop uses remix and storytelling to support cross-cultural dialogue and exchange.

*Participants*: This workshop can appeal to many communities, but is best suited for diverse contexts where participants come from a range of cultural, social and political backgrounds. We recommend that the workshop is run with between 20 and 30 participants.

*Duration*: This workshop takes 2 hours to complete.

*Materials needed:* The technical needs for this workshop are fairly minimal. Participants will need to have pens, colored pencils or markers. Large sheets of paper can be useful as well. All handouts associated with this workshop should be printed out to be available to each participant. All handouts can also be downloaded via the project website at civicimaginationproject.org.

*Space requirements:* All that is needed are tables and chairs, arranged to facilitate small group work and collaboration. The participants will also need space to draw their illustrations.

*Preparation* (what the facilitator should do to prepare): It is helpful if the facilitator prepares by getting a sense of the popular culture content worlds present in the region and communities participating in the workshop. This can help them support the surfacing of content worlds. They will also be better equipped to support participants as they move through the remixing process.

# Running the Workshop

## Icebreaker (15 Minutes)

Ask participants to reflect on their lives and think back to stories that have been meaningful to them. Introduce this process through a brief discussion of why stories matter, how they motivate us, help us find connections to others, and can ultimately help us take action around issues that matter to us. Examples to mention may include stories that have inspired you (have at least two very different examples ready). Stress that the stories should first and foremost be inspirational. They do not need to provide a model for action.

Here is a sample text to use to prompt this process:

*Identify a story that resonates with you and/or your community, that has the potential to inspire people to imagine the future and to think about the actions they can take today in response to that vision.*

*Your story could be a movie, a play, a song, a comic, a myth, a television show, even a commercial. It could be a story that originated in your region, country, town, or it could be a story from somewhere else but that resonates locally. It could be a story that you remember from your childhood. It could be a story that you learned in school, heard at home, or that your friends shared with you. It could be a story that has a much longer cultural tradition behind it. It could even be a story that follows the life of a real person or persons, alive or deceased. They could be celebrities who work to change society, but they also could be everyday folks who do amazing things.*

Ask participants to come up with one story. Then have some of the participants share their story very briefly. List the stories and ideas surfaced on a flipchart or whiteboard to provide all the participants with a starting place for the rest of the workshop.

## Introduction (10 Minutes)

Introduce the participants to storytelling as an important part of our lives. Reviewing the list of stories they surfaced during the ice breaker ask the participants to define storytelling. What makes a good story? What are the key elements of a story? You may choose to use one of the surfaced stories to break down stories, identify characters, plot, conflict, setting and resolution.

## Activity Series

### Inspiring Stories (15 Minutes)

Have each participant write their inspiring story down using the following prompts (use the attached handouts). They should focus on the details of the story and why it matters to them.

> *Inspiring Story Prompt:*
> *Title of your story:*
> *Who are the main characters?*
> *Where does the story take place? When?*
> *What challenges or events occur in the story?*
> *How does the story end?*
> *Why is this story inspiring to you?*

### Connecting Stories (15 Minutes)

Assign participants to small groups (ideally 3 participants per group). Ask each participant to share their inspiring story with their group members. They should briefly narrate their story and then explain why it inspires them. The participants should then discuss what similarities and differences they notice across all the stories that they shared.

### Creating Remixed Story (15 Minutes)

Introduce the idea of remix and mixing stories to create a new one (refer to definition of remix below).

---

**ABOUT REMIX**

Remix is a maker practice used by many individuals and groups. At its most basic level, remix means taking existing content (images, videos, songs, etc.) and transforming that content in some way to create new work. Many powerful remix works comment on the original work, critiquing it or boosting particular elements. However, this is not necessary for a work to be a remix.

---

Ask the participants to come up with a new "remixed" story that uses something (an element) of each of the stories in the group. Possible elements include:

- Themes
- Characters

- Plot
- Locations

Using a handout sheet (one handout per group), ask each group to write down the key elements of their remixed stories.

*Prompt*:

*Title of new story*:
*Title of source stories*:
*Who are the main characters?*
*Where does the story take place? When?*
*What challenges or events occur in the story?*
*How does the story end?*
*Why is this story inspiring to you?*

### Drawing a Visual of the Remixed Story (20 Minutes)

Have the participants design and draw a picture (a visual) that somehow represents their story. It can be a symbol, a character or other visual representation. Make sure they understand that the drawing should help them share their remixed story, it does not need to tell their whole story. Ask them to include the following information on the paper with their drawing/visual:

*Prompt*
*Title of new story*
*Names of team members—who is in your team?*
*What three stories are you drawing on?*

### Sharing Remixed Stories (15 Minutes)

Ask each group to share back their remixed stories. To do this, each group should: stand up, share the individual stories that inspired them, narrate their remixed story, and hold up their drawing as they explain what it means.

> *Note to facilitator: If you are interested in documenting the outcome of this workshop, then consider getting participant permissions to record the presentations and collect the filled out story handouts..*

## Final Reflection (15 Minutes)

Ask the participants to reflect on the process.

What did they enjoy?
What did they notice as they worked to create stories?
What surprised them?
What was difficult?

You may choose to examine one of the remixed stories created during the workshop to demonstrate how going through the remix process allowed the participants to make connections based on what matters to them. In concluding, return to the additive nature of remix, how it helps us think about things differently, and approach stories in new ways. Note that working together to remix stories that matter to us helps us connect with others in surprising ways.

*Facilitator note: We recommend that you collect all materials from the students and suggest that you find a way to share these back with the participants to remind them of the workshop experience.*

# Handouts for Inspiring and Remixed Stories

### Individual Inspiring Story Handout

Title of your story:

Who are the main characters?

Where does the story take place? When?

What challenges or events occur in the story?

How does the story end?

Why is this story inspiring to you?

**Remixed Story Handout**

Title of new story:

Title of source stories:

Who are the main characters?

Where does the story take place? When?

What challenges or events occur in the story?

How does the story end?

Why is this story inspiring to you?

Visual of new story (can be done on separate piece of paper):

# CHAPTER SEVENTEEN

# Creating an Action Plan— Imagining the Process of Change

*We support groups, communities and organizations as they imagine action that will help them accomplish their civic goals.*

## Overview/Intro/Core Idea

We understand that social impact strategies emerge from people's ability to imagine the process of transformation. In this workshop, we explore ways to harness the civic imagination while developing an action plan for social impact. The emphasis here is on being creative and getting inspired, developing strategies for action, and imagining success.

The workshop balances its focus on concrete steps for action with the creative sensibilities and fun of the civic imagination approach. Participants will have the opportunity to map out tentative actions that they think could lead to real world change, while also maintaining a big picture vision of success and possibility. Participants start by identifying issues of concern. Next, they map out strategies and goals that would help them take action around this issue. They then create a profile for an ideal participant/user, as well as a celebrity spokesperson. Finally, they tap their imagination to create a short video that imagines a future scenario where their efforts led to hugely successful outcomes beyond their wildest dreams.

Fig. 17.1. Creating an action plan. Image Credit: Greg Whicker

## Logistics/Nuts and Bolts

*Goal:* This workshop asks participants to envision an action plan for change. They will define issues they care about and come up with specific strategies and goals to set in motion a vision of change, translating imaginative practice into real world action.

*Participants*: Media makers, civic groups, high school students, college students. Group size can range from 10 to 30.

*Duration:* Around 2 hours and 30 minutes or more (duration will fluctuate based on number of participants)

*Materials needed*: paper, markers, smartphones (with ability to shoot video), whiteboards, flip charts, ability to project/share back media created (projector that supports video and audio or large enough video monitor for group playback)

*Space requirements:* Variable, involves large group and break out media making assignments

*Preparation* (what the facilitator should do to prepare): If you are working with local partners be sure to have a conversation with them about cultural and political contexts involved. In addition, you should familiarize yourself with the key concepts featured in this workshop, especially the action strategies described below. Feel free to add to the list if you feel something that is relevant to your context is missing from the list we suggest! Finally, you will need to print out included worksheets, which can also be accessed through www.civicimaginationproject.org.

# Running the Workshop

## Icebreaker (15 Minutes)

To support initial introductions, go around the room and ask participants to go around and to briefly describe a childhood hero of theirs (or a current hero!). This could be someone from their real lives, a celebrity, athlete, fictional character, etc. Ask them to share what this hero meant to them when they were young (or you can also keep it in the present tense), and what qualities made them a hero.

## Introduction (20 Minutes)

Use the idea of personal heroes to transition to talking about personal values and issues and problems facing our communities and the world at large that may be at odds with those values. Explain that in the workshop today we'll be talking about imaginative strategies to tackle those problems.

Introduce the action strategies (inspired by Ethan Zuckerman's 2016 piece, "Effective Civics"). Explain that as participants develop their action plans they'll be asked to apply these strategies. As you go through the strategies one by one, ask participants if they can think of examples from their own experiences that fit into each category. Note that these approaches rarely exist in isolation from each other. We are just discussing them separately within the context of this workshop.

### ACTION STRATEGIES

- **Shifting awareness/norms**—Do people know about the problem you are trying to solve? Are you trying to change their views on a topic? Think about both how your action plan might reach, influence, and educate those who do not know anything about your issue, but also how those who may already have some knowledge and investment in the subject can be empowered by your work with new learning, tools of engagement and clear opportunities for participation and message spreading so that they can build bridges and reach others.
- **Community and network building**—This area can also be closely aligned with awareness building, but rather than emphasizing long term wide-spread shifts in norms, the focus here is on making productive functional connections between communities, groups and networks with mutual values, goals and interests. Are there potential allies currently working in

isolation that your action plan can reach? How will you identify and reach them, and how will you help them to see potential strengths and connections that they haven't seen before? Once connections are made, how will your action plan support new channels of communication, collaboration and productivity?

- **Raising funds/capital**—Will money or other support help solve the issue with which your effort engages? What do you need? Where could the funds and other assets come from and where will they go? How can your action plan help to drive this engagement so that users and audiences feel motivated and good about donating money? Raising capital is not a solution in and of itself, but it may be an important aspect of many different approaches.

- **Market shifts**—Your action plan may look to the world of business for the way it seeks to make change. With contemporary tools, a business can be up and running and reaching people all over the world faster than a government can pass new laws or elections can be held. Market logics can also be applied where existing businesses have stakes or play large roles in the issues your project may wish to address. Corporations can be petitioned and lobbied to change harmful practices or take the lead in positive change. By considering the functions and logics of markets your action plan may consider many different strategic approaches.

- **Policy change**—Is there an institutional change that you are seeking to bring about through your efforts? Are there laws that you would like to enact or repeal? Who are the people in power? Who are their constituents? How have other changes in this area come about and where do you see an opportunity to organize for change in an effective way? What actions can your participants take that will help bring this change about? Whether the change takes place at the local or national level, you need to have a clear plan for what change would look like and who would be ready to sit down at the table with leaders to work together to make that change.

Once you have shared them all, ask the participants to review the 5 action strategies. Encourage them to add any strategies they feel have been left out. If the participants do make suggestions, add these to the list of action strategies by writing them up on the board.

## Activity Series

### *Identifying Issues* (15 Minutes)

Ask participants to collectively create a list of civic concerns that matter to them. The list can be very broad and be sure to let everyone in the room contribute. Areas of concern can be local or global and may include climate change, housing, health, human rights, free speech and many other issues.

Once the list is created, go through a selection process that allows smaller groups (of 3–4 participants) to collaborate on a particular civic issue. You can have people sign up by interest. You can also assign them to groups and have them work within the groups to come up with a topic that is of interest to all there participants. Distribute the Action Plan worksheet to all the groups.

## Issues, Action Strategies and Goals (20 Minutes)

### Narrowing the Issue

Focusing on the civic issue they identified, ask participants to define the problem they face and why it matters to them. If their topic is very broad, ask participants to narrow it down.

*Prompt*

*What is the issue you're tackling? Why is it important to you?*

*If it is a big, complicated issue, can it be broken down into multiple interrelated parts? If so, define those parts and decide where to place your focus.*

### Getting Serious About Strategies and Goals

Once groups have narrowed down their issue, they will spend time getting more specific about their action strategy and goals. What do want to accomplish? What action strategy is most relevant? Articulating the strategies and goals of their action plan at the outset helps the participants identify what matters most in relation to their issue.

*Prompt: Use a scale of 1 to 5 (1= lowest and 5=highest priority) to indicate how relevant each action strategy is to the issue you have identified.*

- *Shifting awareness/norms*
- *Community and Network Building*
- *Raising Capital*
- *Market Shifts*
- *Policy Change*

Now, ask participants to identify 2–3 goals they have in mind as they think about addressing their issue. These goals could be short-term or longterm, but they should grow out of the action strategies that they rated as most relevant to their issue.

*Prompt*:

*Identify 2–3 goals would you would like to meet to address your issue/problem. Your goals should tap your top rated action strategies.*

## Participation Profiles and Celebrity Spokesperson (20 Minutes)

All quests for social impact require bringing people together to help achieve the goals of the action plan.

### Participant Profile

This section is all about creating a detailed profile of the kind of person the participants want to reach with their action. It is important to be very specific about WHO they are trying to reach and how they are hoping this person will participate as this gives them a chance to step back from their own perspectives and really imagine how other people will learn about engage with their issue and action strategy.

#### Participant Profile Prompt

Imagine who you are trying to reach with your action strategy. Imagine who this person is – give them a name. Your imagined participant should be someone who finds out about what you're doing and is instantly hooked. They share it with their friends, they follow every new development, they can't wait for more. As the experience grows they reach out and share their thoughts and reactions. When a call to action is sent they're the first to respond, when challenges are set, they're the first to achieve them. When success is achieved, it's because people like them got involved, accepted the responsibility and role of a true collaborator. They then gave the project a whole new life because they made it their own.

Using the included worksheet, ask the participants to imagine the following characteristics for their ideal participant:

- *Name*
- *Age*
- *Location*
- *Gender identification—male, female, cis, trans, non-conforming?*
- *Relationships—family, friends, romance, many, few, none? What do they do together? Where do they meet?*
- *Work situation and/or school situation*
- *Media diet/Technology—likes and dislikes. What music do they listen to? Books? TV? Movies? Video games?*
- *What matters most to them?*

*Celebrity Spokesperson*

This section gives participants a chance to explore their issue and action strategy through the lens of popular culture as they imagine and describe an ideal celebrity spokesperson. This also gives participants a chance to reflect on the pros and cons of celebrity culture and the power of public platforms. Their ideal celebrity could come from the world of music, sports, television/movies, etc. They should pick someone who they think would reach and inspire the person they profiled above. They can use the included worksheet to answer the following types of questions.

> **Celebrity Spokesperson Prompt**
> *Who is your ideal celebrity spokesperson?*
> *Why are they famous?*
> *How did they get involved in your cause?*
> *How can they help you achieve your goals?*

*Create Success Scenario and Short Video* (30 Minutes)

Drawing on everything they have done so far, ask the participants to take 5 minutes to imagine the big picture and a blue sky vision of success.
*Success scenario prompt:*

- *What if all your wildest ambitions take form? What if things are even better than you ever imagined and your action makes the biggest, world-changing impact possible on the issue you care about?*
- *What would happen? What does success look like? How long does it take?*
- *What are the main events and milestones that you foresee?*
- *What role would your ideal participant and celebrity spokesperson play?*

Next ask participants to pull all this together to collectively create a short mock news story that is set in the future. The news story they create will report on the success of their action plan. The mock news story story should:

- Be maximum 2–3 minutes long
- Include a brief account of what happened. What issue did it address?
- Include a reporter and some of the people behind the campaign
- Should include an interview with a campaign participant (either the celebrity spokesperson or the 'regular' user)
- Should be acted out live as a short skit or recorded and uploaded to YouTube or Vimeo or otherwise shared to be watched by everyone.

The participants will have to create a plan for this story and will have to assign roles for acting it out. Give the participants at least 20 minutes to create their mock news skit before you watch what they created as a group.

## Viewing and Reflection (30 Minutes)

Have all the participants watch all the mock news stories before you ask them to reflect on how imagining success shifted their ideas about the campaign. As the workshop winds down, ask participants to consider how they might be able to turn elements of success scenarios into reality. Ask them to share any ideas they have and resources they know about.

Finally, return to the worksheets to review everything that the participants accomplished in this session and encourage them to continue to find ways to bring imagination into civic action.

# Workshop: Creating an Action Plan—Imagining the Process of Change

## Worksheet

*Issues, Action Strategies and Goals*

### Defining the issue

What is the issue you're tackling? Why is it important to you? If it is a big, complicated issue, can it be broken down into multiple interrelated parts? If so, define those parts and decide where to place your focus.

### Getting serious about strategies and goals

Use a scale of 1 to 5 (1= lowest and 5=highest priority) to indicate how relevant each Action Strategy is to the issue you have identified.

Action Strategies       1   2    3    4    5
Shifting awareness/norms:
Network building:
Raising Capital:
Market shifts:
Policy change:
Other (please specify) :

List of goals. For each goal, indicate type of change based on the above categories.

Goals
1.
2.
3

*Participation Profile and Celebrity Spokesperson*

Imagine who you are trying to reach with your action strategy. Imagine who this person is – give them a name. Your imagined participant should be someone who finds out about what you're doing and is instantly hooked. They share it with their friends, they follow every new development, they can't wait for more. As the experience grows they reach out and share their thoughts and reactions. When a call to action is sent they're the first to respond, when challenges are set, they're the first to achieve them. When success is achieved, it's because people like them got involved, accepted the responsibility and role of a true collaborator. They then gave the project a whole new life because they made it their own.

**Participant Profile**

- *Name*
- *Age*
- *Location*
- *Gender identification—male, female, cis, trans, non-conforming?*
- *Relationships—family, friends, romance, many, few, none? What do they do together? Where do they meet?*
- *Work situation and/or school situation*
- *Media diet/Technology—likes and dislikes. What music do they listen to? Books? TV? Movies? Video games?*
- *What matters most to them?*

**Celebrity Spokesperson**

Who is your ideal celebrity spokesperson? Why are they famous? How did they get involved in your cause? How can they help you achieve your goals?

## Create Success Scenario

What if all your wildest ambitions take form? What if things are even better than you ever imagined and your action makes the biggest, world-changing impact possible on the issue you care about? What would happen? What does success look like? How long does it take? What are the main events and milestones that you foresee? What role would your ideal participant and celebrity spokesperson play?

# Bibliography

Zuckerman, Ethan. 2016. "Effective Civics". In *Civic Media: Technology/Design/Practice*, eds. Eric Gordon and Paul Mihailidis. Cambridge: MIT Press.

# CHAPTER EIGHTEEN

# Stories from the Field

Here we share two brief accounts of civic imagination in action. Our hope is for this book and the tools herein to spark ideas and actions in all kinds of different communities and contexts. The first account is from Jimmeka Anderson about her experience piloting our workshops in North Carolina. As we were finishing our book we enlisted the help of several people around the country to take our instructions as written, run the workshops in their own communities, and report back to us about the experience. This process helped us ensure that we were getting the right points across and that our structures and flow were clear. We were extremely gratified not only for the useful feedback we got, but also by reports of excitement and enjoyment from our pilot facilitators and their participants. We decided to share one such account here to give a sense of how other people are already adapting and using these workshops in their own communities.

In the second account, Emilia Yang and Rogelio Alejandro Lopez (members of the Civic Paths Research group at USC) describe an art installation project that grew out of a site-specific action at the U.S.-Mexico border between San Diego and Tijuana. This example provides a very different illustration of the kinds of work that can be launched from a basis in civic imagination. Rather than recounting a workshop experience, this piece describes a collaboration between university students on opposite sides of the border and their joint effort to spark a sense of shared civic imagination and identity around and across the national boundaries between them, using postcards and photographs as a vehicle for dialog and shared vision.

## Building Community Collaboration with Civic Imagination Workshops by Jimmeka Anderson

*Step into the Looking Glass: Imagining Our Social Connections with a Larger Community* is a great workshop for staff development that builds connections and collaboration with staff members to innovatively approach civic advocacy and activism. The part of the workshop that worked very well with a team of community staff members that I worked with between the ages 24 and 62, was the beginning of the session when everyone identified a content world and shared them with the group. Connections with others were made when individuals began sharing their content worlds and their personal experiences that framed their selections. The instructions were very clear. Instead of doing the initial ice breaker, I altered the ice breaker by writing different pop culture pairs from TV Shows and Movies on labels, such as Fred and Wilma, Marge and Homer, Clair and Cliff Huxtable and many others. The participants had no idea the pop culture character they had on their back and had to ask open ended questions while communicating with participants in the room to find out who they were along with their pair. Many of the participants connected with characters in pop culture and began reminiscing down memory lane. This portion was very engaging with the open group.

*Origin Stories: Imagining Ourselves as Civic Agents* was my favorite session to facilitate. This is a great workshop for staff development with adults that allows the team to discover how their pasts builds upon their strengths. Teams discover how everyone's strengths can help to solve problems collaboratively. In preparation for the workshop, I prepared a PowerPoint and handout that I think helped to make everything run smoothly. Participants were very engaged as they shared stories connected to their memory objects. The stories that were shared were heartfelt and some were very funny. Considering that my group is a staff team that were using the Civic Imagination sessions for staff development, I think that it helped the group connect with each other on a deeper level. One of the participants at the end of the session stated that she realized her coworkers and herself possessed many commonalities through everyone's childhood memories. Additionally, in preparation for the session, I printed out approximately 50 memory objects from the 60s, 70s, 80s, and 90s. I cut them out as cards and spread them across the table. I allowed participants to select an object that jogged a memory. Everyone ended up selecting and connecting a memory to objects that they found and wanted to grab more than one memory object out of the card pile.

In conclusion, the Civic Imagination Workshops were fun to facilitate and built innovative ideas while fostering community collaboration with participants. I strongly recommend the workshops to be implemented in schools, community centers and libraries to encourage dialogue with citizens about our society. The workshops are creatively designed to encourage group collaboration with brainstorming ideas for our future world and solving tough problems that may arise together!

## Postcards from/at *Donde Rebotan Los Sueños* [Where Dreams Hit the Wall] by Rogelio Alejandro Lopez and Emilia Yang

Postcards from/at *Donde Rebotan Los Sueños* is an installation composed of an assemblage of pictures and video interviews that traces both real and imagined immigration and border experiences of both sides of the wall that divides Tijuana and San Diego. Each component is an exploration of how project collaborators and people at the site feel this division, becoming a multi-voiced shifting mosaic of ways to consider and live the border. Opening up intersubjective exchanges through dialogues and encounters, the installation is a place for people to wander in and respond to a landscape of images, ideas, and stories about the border wall.

Growing out of a collaboration with Univision's Fusion brand, this project aimed to capitalize on the attention directed at the US-Mexico border, an ongoing global refugee crisis, and Donald Trump's racist and xenophobic 2016 election campaign through a benefit concert called "Rise Up As One". In a political climate where a presidential candidate mobilized his base through an alarmist and nativist discourse, calling for mass deportations and insisting on a crisis along the southern border, the goal of our research team and collaborators was to document the lived experiences of those directly affected by the U.S.-Mexico border and its policies, including communities in the United States and Mexico. Such an effort required an international partnership between students and educators in Tijuana from Iberoamericana University México and Los Angeles from USC.

Challenging the wall's attempt to divide people and cultures that permeate it, our first phase consisted of Mexican students in Tijuana documenting life along the border and the physical structure itself with photography, as a means to create a bi-national dialogue about its impact on envisioning the world. Our student partners photographed that which is often overlooked- the casual ways people live along the border, the artisan communities making a living from cross-border traffic, and recently arrived refugees (from Haiti and countless other places) forging meaning and community despite displacement. These photographs, and their powerful imagery and symbolism, served as the substance for an international dialogue when shown to the attendees of Univision's "Rise Up As One" concert in San Diego, California.

The photographs created by our Mexican partners, which were transnational in nature despite only traveling mere miles northward, became "postcards" and were presented to attendees of the Rise Up As One event. Researchers from USC's Civic Paths presented the postcards to concertgoers inviting them to interpret the images and to share their own experiences with life along the border. They also were able to send messages to the student photographers that took the pictures. Responses ranged from stories about families separated by deportation, to what the wall itself symbolizes in terms of dreams and aspirations. One photograph in particular evoked the strongest emotions and reactions, which depicted the border wall with the words "Aquí es donde rebotan los sueños/This is where dreams hit the wall". As with the art installation itself, we used the concept of the civic imagination ("What is the civic imagination?" https://www.civicimaginationproject.org) to guide our dialogue and to facilitate a speculative space for the border, teasing out aspirations and fears for the future.

*In collaboration with Andrea Alarcon, Linda Artola, Luciana Chamorro, Viviana Bernal, TJ Billard, Elsa Alejandra del Callejo, Ana Luz Duarte, Yomna Elsayed, Brooklyne Gipson, Henry Jenkins, Sara Jiménez, Molly Jones, Rogelio Alejandro López, Pablo Martínez Zárate, Miguel Parro, Gabriel Peters-Lazaro, Paola Saracho, Sangita Shresthova, Gustavo Vargas, Emilia Yang, Sulafa Zidani*

## Bibliography

De Michiel, H., & Zimmerman, P. 2013. Documentary as Open Space. *The Documentary Film Book*, 355–365.

Gaudenzi, S. 2013. *The living documentary: From representing reality to co-creating reality in digital interactive documentary* (Doctoral dissertation, Goldsmiths, University of London).

Jenkins, Henry, Sangita Shresthova, Liana Gamber-Thompson, and Neta Kligler-Vilenchik. 2016. "Superpowers to the People! How Young Activists Are Tapping the Civic Imagination." In *Civic Media: Technology, Design, Practice,* eds. Eric Gordon and Paul Mihailidis. Cambridge, MA: MIT. 295–320.

# Final Thoughts

Though many things have changed in the world around us since we began our focus on civic imagination in 2013, we recognize that our core principles and motivations continue to ring true. In many ways, the urgency we feel around the need for the civic imagination has grown. In fact, as we have been finishing this manuscript and reflecting on final thoughts that we might share, we see many examples in the worlds of popular culture and politics that affirm these needs and perhaps mark a larger shift towards creative visions of hope as vital forms of civic engagement. From the imaginative social movements inspired by the release of the *Black Panther* film in 2018 to a 2019 animated video called "A message from the future with Alexandria Ocasio-Cortez" that envisions a more equitable and environmentally sustainable future, we see ample evidence that others recognize that we need to bring active imagination to our individual and collective civic lives. Whether it is an invitation to "dream Wakanda" or recognizing that the "first step [towards our desired future] was just closing our eyes and imagining it" (Alexandra Ocasio Cortez), such efforts center imagination as a key aspect of our ability to engage with others as we advocate for changing our circumstances. It is our hope that the workshops we share here can support others in their efforts to bring the imagination to their civic lives.

With that in mind, we felt it would be helpful to share a few final thoughts about some themes that emerged from the Imagine2040 symposium of 2017 (an event that we touch upon in the introduction to this book). As we reviewed them two years later, these three themes stuck out to us as an enduring and useful place to conclude our book and extend an invitation to our readers to engage with our workshops. These themes emerged from discussions with participants and were summarized by members of our research team as indicated below.

First, engaging the imagination is not escapism, it is a necessary escape. Imagination is an active process. Though the act of imagining can initially feel passive, it is an opportunity to process, to move beyond physical limitations. The imagination allows us to experiment and move beyond accepted constraints. Imagining is not the opposite of taking real world action. Rather, it expands our spectrum of what we mean by taking civic action. Imagining as escape in itself can be a retreat, a moment to reflect, make sense of the world and imagine alternatives. Imagination becomes a necessity when reality is filled with constraints and challenges. Once imagination is actionable, it is transformed from being an escapist route to becoming an escape route. (Based on summary by Yomna Elsayed)

Second, the imagination is both a mechanism and valence of civic action. Imaginations shift in civic meaning when they are shared. When imagination is shared, it moves from the private space of our own minds to a shared public space in which it is engaged in conversation. A sense of collectivity is a necessary means, part of the mechanism of any civic imagining, but it is not an ethical end. Ethical civic imaginations must be built on the fact that there are and will be important differences between people—there will always be people fighting for what they believe in. (Based on summary by Samantha Close)

Third, to imagine a civic world, you must also imagine how change happens and how power can operate. It is essential to imagine power: what it is and where it comes from. There does not need to be only one kind or source of power, but knowing what they are and how they are accessed is essential. (Based on summary by Samantha Close)

By developing workshop methodologies that engage these key themes, we hope that our efforts have confirmed the value of the imagination as a collective practice of strengthening shared values and taking action to realize and nurture them in our larger world. As one of our Imagine2040 participants summarized it, the civic imagination is "about a combination of responsibility and dreaming and I think that that's something very powerful and very needed. There is this sense that dreaming has a place and that figuring out a smarter and saner path forward is more important now than ever." We hope that the stories and tools in this book will encourage people to take time to imagine a better world together, and then to work together to realize those hopes, dreams and values.

# Recommended Readings

We offer the following recommendations for anyone interested in a deeper dive into the literature that has informed the scholarly aspects of our work. As stated in the introduction, this book's focus is on practice, but that practice emerges from an extensive history of research and writing. Interested readers might first consult the other publications coming from our team, including *By Any Media Necessary*, and *Popular Culture and the Civic Imagination* (bibliographic details included below). Our websites, byanymedia.net and civicimaginationproject.org also contain writing and links that may be of interest.

To provide further guidance we have organized our reading sections below into four broad categories: Participatory Cultures and Connected Learning, Participatory Politics, Imagination, Pedagogy and Future Aesthetics, and Memory and Nostalgia. The recommended readings in each category are by no means exhaustive. Rather we try to highlight key texts that have been useful to us, and that we believe will provide excellent foundations or jumping off points for readers.

Jenkins, Henry, Sangita Shresthova, Liana Gamber-Thompson, Neta Kligler-Vilenchik, and Arely Zimmerman. 2016. *By Any Media Necessary: The New Youth Activism*. New York: NYU Press.

Jenkins, Henry, Gabriel Peters-Lazaro, Sangita Shresthova, editors. 2020. *Popular Culture and the Civic Imagination: Case Studies of Creative Social Change*. New York: NYU Press.

# Participatory Cultures and Connected Learning

We enter into civics and politics through cultural engagement, specifically practices associated participatory cultures. Drawing on Henry Jenkins' et al. (2006, v) seminal work on New Media Literacies we define participatory cultures as those with:

1.  With relatively low barriers to artistic expression and civic engagement
2.  With strong support for creating and sharing one's creations with others
3.  With some type of informal mentorship whereby what is known by the most experienced is passed along to novices
4.  Where members believe that their contributions matter
5.  Where members feel some degree of social connection with one another (at the least they care what other people think about what they have created).

Not every member must contribute, but all must believe they are free to contribute when ready and that what they contribute will be appropriately valued.

As we highlight the participatory potential of such cultural contexts, we also remain cognizant of their 'real world' negotiations and constraints. As Henry Jenkins suggests in his dialogue with Nico Carpentier (2013), this definition of participatory culture may, in fact, "be a utopian goal, meaningful in the ways that it motivates our struggles to achieve it and provides yardsticks to measure what we've achieved."

Our previous work sought to more clearly define these "yardsticks" as they relate to participation in cultural spaces. In particular, we were interested in how organizations and networks encourage youth to more meaningfully participate in civic and political life by building on existing cultural interests and affinities. As Peter Dahlgren (2011) aptly observes "One has to feel invited, committed and/or empowered to enter into a participatory process." Our civic imagination workshops, highlight practices that support sociality, or a sense of social connection that mediates ties formed through what Mizuko Ito et al. identify as friendship-driven and interest driven activities (2009) that support connected learning (2019).

Brough, Melissa and Sangita Shresthova. 2012. "Fandom Meets Activism: Rethinking Civic and Political Participation". Transformative Works and Cultures. Vol 10. https://doi.org/10.3983/twc.2012.0303

Carpentier, Nico and Henry Jenkins. 2013. "Theorizing Participatory Intensities: A Conversation About Participation and Politics." *Convergence* 19(3) (August): 265–286.

Dahlgren, Peter. 2011. "Parameters of Online Participation: Conceptualising Civic Contingencies." *Communication Management Quarterly* (6)21: 87–110.

Jenkins, Henry. 2006. *Confronting the Challenges of Participatory Culture: Media Education for the 21st Century.* John D. and Catherine T. MacArthur Foundation, Chicago, 5–7, 19–20, 3–4.

Ito, Mizuko et al. 2019. *Affinity Online: How Connection and Shared Interest Fuel Learning.* New York: NYU Press.

Ito, Mizuko et al. 2009. *Hanging Out, Messing Around and Geeking Out: Kids Living and Learning with New Media.* Cambridge: MIT Press.

Kido, Lopez Lori. 2016. *Asian American Media Activism: Fighting for Cultural Citizenship.* New York: NYU Press.

## Participatory Politics

Though not every text in this section is explicitly about participatory politics, each provides crucial insight into the complex interlocking concepts that inform our understanding of the term. Participatory politics is the framework through which we understand contemporary civic and political conditions. Our team came to this work mainly from the adjacent subject of participatory culture, as described by Jenkins et al. (2006). Within our contemporary environment, participation in the political process is not just about traditional interactions with formal institutions. Familiar acts like voting or attending city council meetings are still important, but the spheres of public discourse also include social media and popular culture. Participatory politics includes all kinds of peer to peer interactions in which people are attempting to influence and interact with diverse areas of concern within their communities, whether on a local, national or global scale. Scholars participating in the MacArthur Foundation-supported Youth and Participatory Politics Research network (of which our team was a part) produced excellent resources for teaching and learning about the ways young people experience political participation in contemporary life (see Cohen & Kahne 2012 and https://ypp.dmlcentral.net/).

Other related works that inform our thinking in this area but may not be explicitly about participatory politics include the works of Benedict Anderson (2006) and Henri Lefebvre, which provide foundations for how we think about the social and cultural constructions of communities and public space. In *Civic Imagination: Making a Difference in American Political Life,* Baiocchi et al. adopt a sociological perspective for doing fieldwork on a range of local organizations in hopes of identifying the informal models of political change animating their work. Haiven and Khasnabish (2014) focus on 'the radical imagination' as a way of framing and understanding their work about and with activist groups in Canada.

*Beautiful Trouble: A Toolbox for Revolution*, by Andrew Boyd and David Oswald Mitchell, is even more practice focused and collects accounts of best practices of contemporary activists working within grassroots contexts. Matt Ratto and Meghan Boler's *DIY Citizenship: Critical Making and Social Media*, and Eric Gordon and Paul Mihailidis's *Civic Media: Technology, Design, Practice*, explore some similar ground but are aimed more squarely at readers from specific academic disciplines. Amber Day's *DIY Utopia: Cultural Imagination and the Remaking of the Possible* is comprised of a collection of articles that situate the do-it-yourself movement within a contemporary utopian—anti-mainstream—ethos. Davide Panagia's *Ten Theses For An Aesthetics of Politics* maps the relations between the art world and the political sector, offering an abstract conceptual model that accounts for the consciousness-raising potential of creative work.

Anderson, Benedict. 2006. *Imagined Communities: Reflections on the Origin and Spread of Nationalism*. London: Verso.

Baiocchi, Gianpaolo, Elizabeth A. Bennett, Alissa Cordner, Peter Taylor Klein, and Stephanie Savell. 2014. *The Civic Imagination: Making a Difference in American Political Life*. New York: Routledge.

Boyd, Andrew, & Mitchell, Dave Oswald. 2016. *Beautiful Trouble a Toolbox for Revolution*. New York: Or Books.

Cohen, Cathy J. and Joseph Kahne. 2012. "Participatory Politics: New Media and Youth Political Action." MacArthur Foundation Youth and Participatory Politics Research Network (June). https://ypp.dmlcentral.net/sites/default/files/publications/Participatory_Politics_Report.pdf

Gordon, Eric and Paul Mihailidis. 2016. *Civic Media: Technology, Design, Practice*. Cambridge: MIT Press.

Jenkins, Henry et al. 2006. *Confronting the Challenges of Participatory Culture: Media Education for the 21st Century*. John D. and Catherine T. MacArthur Foundation, Chicago.

Lefevbre, Henri. 1991. *The Production of Space*. Cambridge, MA: Blackwell.

Ratto, Matt and Boler, Megan. 2014. *DIY Citizenship: Critical Making and Social Media*. Cambridge: The MIT Press.

## Imagination, Pedagogy and Future Aesthetics

One of the key texts to inspire our civic imagination work is Stephen Duncombe's *Dream: Re-Imagining Progressive Politics in an Age of Fantasy*, which sought to demonstrate the value of ethical spectacle, including political street theater, and to urge activists to seek inspiration from Madison Avenue, Las Vegas, and the games industry. Duncombe's more recent works contribute to a deeper understanding of the role of critical utopias in proposing alternatives to contemporary political realities and introduced the concept of "the tyranny of the possible" which helps inform the need to move beyond realist rhetorics. In *Dream*, Duncombe talks about the kinds of narrative and media practices that might be leveraged for new kinds of political action. Our work is concerned with a similar approach in terms of identifying and connecting new kinds of practice to civic and political movements. For us, that move to practice is grounded in imagination and pedagogy, and opens up to include aspects of design, media arts and speculative fiction.

Maxine Greene's work, *Releasing the Imagination* (1995) is an excellent place to start in terms of framing imagination as an active process of collective creativity and action that can contribute to social change. One of her areas of emphasis is on education. We also see education and teaching as key components to the civic imagination approach and have found Paulo Freire's seminal work, *Pedagogy of the Oppressed*, to be a valuable resource in this regard. Freire explores the relationships between language, literacy, oppression and power, and details ways in which pedagogy can be a tool for emancipation and solidarity and a vehicle towards the realization of radical real world change. Along these lines, Ernest Morell's works apply many of Freire's lessons to contemporary practices of media production as vernacular language of youth culture. With pedagogy as our bridge to practice, there are several disciplinary approaches that inform the kinds of creative work we connect with civic imagination. Worldbuilding is high amongst this list, and our approach is directly informed by collaboration with Alex McDowell who describes his methodology in "Prejudicial Narratives: Building Tomorrow's World Today" and in "World Building and the Future of Media: A Case Study-Makoko 2036" with Cechanowicz and Cantrell. McDowell's worldbuilding can be framed within larger trends of speculative design as described in works by Bleecker (2009), Pendleton-Jullian and Brown (2016), and Dunne and Raby (2013).

Many of these qualities—future-focused creative practices as a means of advancing an emancipatory political project—converge in the phenomenon of Afrofuturism. In *Freedom Dreams: the Black Radical Imagination*, Kelley uses personal experiences to frame an in-depth history of the political struggles of African Americans with an extended exploration of afrofuturism as a multidisciplinary artistic phenomenon envisioning a better future. Womack (2013) provides an extended examination of afrofuturism in science fiction and fantasy, and *Octavia's Brood* is an excellent collection of short stories combine activist visions with science fiction narratives in an homage to the author Octavia Butler.

Bleecker, Julian. 2009. "Design Fiction: A Short Essay on Design, Science, Fact and Fiction." *Near Future Laboratory*. http://drbfw5wfjlxon.cloudfront.net/writing/DesignFiction_WebEdition.pdf

Brown, Adrienne Maree and Walidah Imarisha, eds.. 2015. *Octavia's Brood: Science Fiction Stories From Social Justice Movements*. Oakland: AK Press.

Cechanowicz, Laura, Brian Cantrell, and Alex McDowell. 2016. "Worldbuilding and the Future of Media: A Case Study-Makoko 2036" *IEEE Technology and Society Magazine* Volume: 35(4) (December): 28–38.

Duncombe, Stephen. 2007. *Dream: Re-imagining Progressive Politics in an Age of Fantasy*. New York: The New Press.

Dunne, Anthony, and Fiona, Raby. 2013. *Speculative Everything: Design, Fiction, and Social Dreaming*. Cambridge: MIT Press.

Freire, Paulo. 2000. *Pedagogy of the Oppressed*. New York: Continuum.

Greene, Maxine. 1995. *Releasing the Imagination: Essays on Education, the Arts, and Social Change*. San Francisco: Jossey Bass.

Haiven, Max, and Alex Khasnabish. 2014. *The Radical Imagination: Social Movement Research in the Age of Austerity*. London: Zed Books.

Kelley, Robin D. G. 2002. *Freedom Dreams: The Black Radical Imagination*. Boston: Beacon Press.

McDowell, Alex. 2015. "Prejudicial Narratives: Building Tomorrow's World Today." *Architectural Design*, vol. 85(4): 26–33.

Morrell, Ernest. 2008. *Critical Literacy and Urban Youth: Pedagogies of Access, Dissent, and Liberation*. New York: Routledge.

Morrell, Ernest. 2013. *Critical Media Pedagogy: Teaching for Achievement in City Schools*. New York: Teachers College Press.

Panagia, Davide. 2016. *Ten Theses for an Aesthetics of Politics*. Minneapolis: University of Minnesota Press.

Pendleton-Jullian, Ann and John Seely Brown. 2016. *Pragmatic Imagination: Prequel to Design Unbound*. San Francisco: Blurb.

Womack, Ytasha. 2013. *Afrofuturism: The world of black sci-fi and fantasy culture*. Chicago: Chicago Review Press.

## Memory and Nostalgia

While many of these examples highlight the future-focused nature of the civic imagination work, we also understand and have benefited from exploring the importance of historical perspectives. Within historical examples, we also encountered what we might consider the dark side of the civic imagination; times when practices that share some similarities with civic imagination were used to promulgate and enact a vision of the world that restricted rather than enhanced democratic participation and personal freedoms for diverse citizenry. The writings of Hannah

Arendt (1966) on totalitarianism in Nazi Germany and Stalin's USSR are a clarion warning of the destructive power of such visions. Václav Havel's (1990) work on the post-totalitarian condition in the Soviet controlled Eastern Europe expands Arendt's work to examine how oppression transforms as totalitarian regimes transition to exercising power through the mundane and everyday practices. Boym (2002) examines the power of nostalgia for imaginary pasts and places to inform our contemporary choices. Klein (2017) ties many of these threads together in her critiques and warnings of the current state of U.S. politics, and Cornell and Seely (2017) link similar ideas to a longer history in philosophy, emphasizing concepts from Spinoza to help define positive terms for the expansion of diversity and freedom as requisites for the advancement of democracy.

Arendt, Hannah. 1966. *The Origins of Totalitarianism*. New York: Harcourt, Brace & World.

Boym, Svetlana. 2002 *The Future of Nostalgia*. New York: Basic Books.

Cornell, Drucilla and Stephen D. Seely. 2017. "What Happened to the Public Imagination, and Why?," global-e, March 21, http://www.21global.ucsb.edu/global-e/march-2017/what-has-happened-public-imagination-and-why

Havel, Václav. 1990. *Disturbing the Peace: A Conversation with Karel Hvížďala* (Paul Wilson, Trans.) New York: Alfred A. Knopf.

Klein, Naomi. 2017. *No Is Not Enough: Resisting Trump's Politics and Winning the World We Need*. Chicago: Haymarket Books.

Miller, Daniel. 2009. *The Comfort of Things*. New York: Polity Press.

# Author Biographies

Gabriel Peters-Lazaro is an Assistant Professor of Practice at the USC School of Cinematic Arts where he researches, designs and produces digital media for innovative learning. Through the Hypercinemas Research Group he investigates the continuities between emerging technologies of representation and the earliest experiments of cinema in order to transcend spectacle and achieve a material understanding of current tools and how they can support a critically engaged cinematic practice. He helped create The Junior AV Club, an action research project that explored mindful media making and sharing as powerful practices of early childhood learning. As a member of the advisory board of LA Makerspace he helps to bring innovative learning explorations to youth in Los Angeles through the public library system. As a producer and cinematographer he recently completed a feature length documentary on assisted reproductive technologies (ART) called *One More Shot*. He teaches courses for undergraduate and graduate students dealing with critical media making and theory. He received his B.A. in Film Studies from UC

Berkeley, completed his M.F.A in Film Directing and Production at UCLA and his Ph.D. at USC in Cinematic Arts.

**Sangita Shresthova** is the Director of Research of the Civic Paths Group based at the University of Southern California. Her work focuses on intersections among online learning, popular culture, performance, new media, politics, and globalization. She is also one of the authors of *Popular Culture and the Civic Imagination: Case Studies of Creative Change* (2020) and of *By Any Media Necessary: The New Activism of Youth* (2016), both published by NYU Press. Her earlier book on Bollywood (*Is It All About Hips?*) was published in 2011 by Sage. She is one of the creators of the Digital Civics Toolkit (digitalcivicstoolkit.org), a collection of resources for educators, teachers and community leaders to support youth learning. Her own creative work has been presented in academic and creative venues around the world including the Schaubuehne (Berlin), the Other Festival (Chennai), the EBS International Documentary Festival (Seoul), and the American Dance Festival (Durham, NC). She enjoys engaging with diverse communities through her workshops, lectures and projects.

**Foreword Author Biography:**

**Henry Jenkins** is the Provost's Professor of Communication, Journalism, Cinematic Arts and Education at the University of Southern California. His previous books include *Convergence Culture: Where Old and New Media Collide* and *Spreadable Media: Creating Meaning and Value in a Networked Society* (with Sam Ford and Joshua Green).

**Notes from the Field Contributor Biographies:**

**Jimmeka Anderson** is a Doctoral student in the Urban Education program at the University of North Carolina at Charlotte with a focus on adolescents and media. Currently, Jimmeka resides in Charlotte, NC where she has served as the Founder and Executive Director of I AM not the Media, Inc. for six years, a non-profit organization for teens that empowers youth through media literacy and media creation (www.iamnotthemedia.org) and is the Chapter Lead for North Carolina for the national Media Literacy Now organization. In her current position at Charlotte Mecklenburg Library, Jimmeka serves as a Library Coordinator where she plans outreach programs throughout the city of Charlotte, NC.

**Rogelio Alejandro Lopez** is a Ph.D. candidate at the Annenberg School for Communication and Journalism at the University of Southern California, where his work centers on social movements, civic media, and youth culture. His dissertation is a comparative look into the role of media strategies and cultural production in developing a civic imagination among contemporary youth social movements.

**Emilia Yang** is an activist, artist, and militant researcher. Yang is currently a Ph.D. student in Media Arts + Practice in the School of Cinematic Arts at the University of Southern California. Her work has been interconnected with digital communications, performance, and public art. Her research focuses on participatory culture and its relationship to media, arts, and design. Her art practice utilizes site-specific interactive installations, interactive documentaries, performance, and urban interventions, all of which explore social justice issues in participatory ways.

# Index

new
literacies
¶

AND DIGITAL EPISTEMOLOGIES

Colin Lankshear & Michele Knobel

*General Editors*

New literacies emerge and evolve apace as people from all walks of life engage with new technologies, shifting values and institutional change, and increasingly assume 'postmodern' orientations toward their everyday worlds. Despite many efforts to take account of such changes, educational institutions largely remain out of touch with the range of new ways of making and sharing meanings that increasingly mediate and shape the lives of the young people they teach and the futures they face. This series aims to explore some key dimensions of the changes occurring within social practices of literacy and the educational challenges they present, with a view to informing educational practice in helpful ways. It asks what are new literacies, how do they impact on life in schools, homes, communities, workplaces, sites of leisure, and other key settings of human cultural engagement, and what significance do new literacies have for how people learn and how they understand and construct knowledge. It aims to challenge established and 'official' ways of framing literacy, and to ask what it means for literacies to be powerful, effective, and enabling under current and foreseeable conditions. Collectively, the works in this series will help to reorient literacy debates and literacy education agendas.

For further information about the series and submitting manuscripts, please contact:

Michele Knobel & Colin Lankshear
Montclair State University
Dept. of Education and Human Services
3173 University Hall
Montclair, NJ 07043
michele@coatepec.net

To order other books in this series, please contact our Customer Service Department:

peterlang@presswarehouse.com (within the U.S.)
order@peterlang.com (outside the U.S.)

Or browse online by series at: www.peterlang.com